TREES
AND HOW TO GROW THEM

THE TREE
COUNCIL

MARGARET LIPSCOMBE AND JON STOKES

First published 2008 by Think Books
an imprint of Pan Macmillan Ltd
Pan Macmillan, 20 New Wharf Road, London N1 9RR
Basingstoke and Oxford
Associated companies throughout the world
www.panmacmillan.com
www.think-books.com

ISBN 978-1-84525-060-7

Text Copyright: Pan Macmillan Ltd, Think Publishing and The Tree Council
Design Copyright: Think Publishing
Authors: Margaret Lipscombe and Jon Stokes of The Tree Council
Editor: Malcolm Tait
Deputy editor: Marion Thompson
Design: Peter Bishop
Photography: Margaret Lipscombe, Edward Parker and Jon Stokes
Illustrations: Lizzie Harper, Graham Reed and John White

Think Books: Tania Adams, Jes Stanfield
With thanks to Richard Jinks and Peter Gosling of Forest Research, Forestry Commission.
Thanks to John White for reading through the text, and to the staff and garden users of
St Mary's Secret Garden, Hackney.

1 3 5 7 9 8 6 4 2

A CIP catalogue record for this book is available from the British Library.

Printed and Bound in Italy by Printer Trento

Visit www.panmacmillan.com to read more about all our books and to buy
them. You will also find features, author interviews and news of any
author events, and you can sign up for e-newsletters so that you're
always first to hear about our new releases.

Cover image: Oak tree © Ian West, Oxford Scientific

The paper in this book comes from well managed forests, independently
certified in accordance with the rules of the Forest Stewardship Council.

I never saw a discontented tree.
They grip the ground as though
they liked it, and though fast rooted
they travel about as far as we do.
John Muir, environmentalist

I think that I shall never see
A billboard lovely as a tree.
Perhaps unless the billboards fall,
I'll never see a tree at all.
Ogden Nash, humorist

THE TREE
COUNCIL

Contents

From the top

Well-known gardener Dan Pearson explains why this book is so timely.

Trees shape our landscape, our memories and our future, and everyone can recall a tree from childhood. The house I grew up in sat on the brow of a wooded hill. Hill Cottage was surrounded by trees: the towering trunks of the Scots pines glowing orange in the light of the setting sun; the primrose yellow catkins on the pussy willows releasing clouds of dusty pollen; the delicate blossom on the bird cherries announcing the arrival of spring; and the spreading branches of the huge turkey oak – planted by the previous owner as a girl – which creaked and brushed my bedroom window in the wind. These trees were also my playground and initiated a passion that has lasted into adulthood – and I am proud to be part of a resurgence of interest in this fascinating world.

Trees are far more than just large, woody plants. Their size and longevity make them an integral part of the living landscape that surrounds us; as important and seemingly permanent as earth, sea and sky. Their roles as complete ecosystems within themselves, as the lungs that keep the atmosphere breathable and as a truly sustainable resource are now more fully understood than ever before. Recently, their ability to soften the ever-hardening urban landscape has brought their importance into focus for a whole new generation of city dwellers. As such, trees have a gravity, significance and influence over us, unlike any other living organism.

As this book goes to print, The Tree Council's Seed Gathering Season is now in its 10th year and it has succeeded in its mission to demonstrate how easy and how much fun it is to grow trees from seed. A fundamental part of the scheme is the growing of trees from locally collected seed. This has huge benefits, since trees of local provenance are already successfully adapted to the local environment. Consequently, they are far more likely to flourish, making it easier to reinstate and beautify local urban and rural spaces. Collecting seed and growing trees is also

Dan Pearson trained at the RHS Garden Wisley and the Royal Botanic Gardens, Kew, before starting his professional career as a designer in 1987. He is also a weekly gardening columnist for The Observer Magazine, *joint author with Sir Terence Conran of* The Essential Garden Book *and author of* The Garden: A year at Home Farm. *He has presented and appeared in TV series on BBC2, Channel 4 and Channel 5 and has designed five award-winning Chelsea Flower Show gardens.*

a great way to get children involved with and connected to nature.

I was delighted to find such a wealth of information in this book. It is an educational tool suitable for children and adults alike. Anyone can befriend and nurture a tree, whether for fruit, blossom, foliage, bark or shade, even in the smallest garden. Here there is a wealth of pages to help identify and illuminate even the most humble British natives. There is a selection of exotic trees too, all of which can equip us for the adjustments we may have to make as a result of climate change. All the information you need to successfully grow all of these trees from seed is here. Start today!

In the studio

Dan Pearson Studio handles a wide range of projects internationally for private and public clients, comprising private gardens, public spaces, architectural landscaping, public parks and civic plantings.

Its work is characterised by an instinctive response to the sense of place resulting in the creation of unique site-specific environments. Of principal importance are the relationships between spaces and the creation of holistic environments with distinctive moods. Primary consideration is given to the boundaries between interior and exterior space, the seating of buildings within landscape and the dialogue between ornamental garden spaces and the wider landscape. A key strength of the studio's designs lies in a simple foundation of hard landscaping intended to create comfortable, usable spaces that are overlaid with loose, bold and painterly naturalistic plantings.

Making trees matter

Since the 1990s, The Tree Council's annual Seed Gathering Season has encouraged people up and down the country to grow trees from seed. And that's not all it does...

The Tree Council is the lead UK tree-campaigning charity, an umbrella body for over 180 organisations working to promote the importance of trees within the changing environment. It works towards:

- making trees matter to everyone

- more trees, of the right kind, in the right places
- better care for all trees, of all ages
- inspiring effective action for trees.

Fundamental to The Tree Council's work are its Community Action Programme and

its nationwide network of Tree Wardens who spearhead this programme (see page 246).

Tree Council members range from voluntary and community organisations, professional and trade associations and non-departmental government bodies to local authorities and key government departments, all concerned with trees, biodiversity and the environment in general.

The Tree Council works with its members on particular issues of concern, such as the Green Monuments Campaign – a major drive for proper safeguards for heritage trees – and the Hedge Tree Campaign to get more trees growing in Britain's hedges.

Community Action Programme

Every year The Tree Council mounts its national Community Action Programme – a calendar of initiatives aimed at involving as many people as possible in planting, caring for and enjoying trees and woods. Events include:

- Seed Gathering Season
- National Tree Week
- Tree Care Campaign
- Walk in the Woods.

Tree Council member organisations, as well as Tree Wardens, are all heavily involved in the Community Action Programme, helping The Tree Council reach out to large groups of people and ensuring maximum activity throughout the country. Schools and community groups that have received funds for tree planting through The Tree Council's grants programme are all encouraged to organise fun and worthwhile events for National Tree Week, as well as the other initiatives.

Seed Gathering Season

Through this autumn festival The Tree Council aims to inspire everyone, particularly schoolchildren and families, to gather seeds, fruits and nuts and grow the trees of the future. The festival starts on 23 September (the autumn equinox, considered to be the first day of autumn) and continues until 23 October, giving everyone plenty of days on which to hold events.

Growing trees from seeds found nearby can have great benefits in restocking areas with trees of local provenance – trees that are adapted to regional circumstances, so are likely to flourish and help restore, conserve and beautify urban and rural spaces. Collecting seeds and growing trees is also a great way to get children involved and start growing the next generation of tree enthusiasts.

National Tree Week

National Tree Week has been organised by The Tree Council since 1975. A festival to mark the start of the tree-planting season, it takes place every year at the end of November/beginning of December.

Tree Week is now the UK's largest annual tree celebration. Its aim is to raise awareness of trees and encourage tree planting and good management. Voluntary bodies, local authorities, schools, Tree Wardens and many other individuals and organisations support the week by arranging local events, inspiring upward of a quarter of a million people to get involved throughout the UK.

About a million trees are planted during the week, and in 2000 a Guinness World Record was set for tree planting by hand – 107,781 over a three-day period.

Since it began, more than 20 million trees have been planted for National Tree Week.

Tree Care Campaign

The Tree Council's national Tree Care Campaign runs from March to September and highlights the need for better care for all trees in order to ensure their survival and increase the number reaching maturity.

It was launched in 1999 to highlight the need for anyone who has planted trees in the past five years to revisit them and carry out a few simple tree-care tasks, such as clearing weeds, mulching and checking ties. These actions can save young trees from dying and allow them to develop into the mature trees that enhance our urban and rural landscape.

Walk in the Woods

This annual Tree Council festival aims to encourage everyone to enjoy trees and woods in spring, when they are particularly attractive. Across the UK, walks, talks and other events take place in town and countryside throughout May – a great month to go down to the woods or to a local park, or to just enjoy tree-lined streets.

Grants Programme

The Tree Council's tree planting grants help schools and communities to improve their environment and learn about the importance of trees. This ensures that children under the age of 16 are given the opportunity to get some hands-on experience of tree planting, creating a new generation of tree enthusiasts with pride in the improvements they have made to their local ground.

For more information please visit www.treecouncil.org.uk.

Grid expectations

National Grid has worked closely with The Tree Council since the early 1990s. Here's your chance to read all about it.

National Grid is an international electricity and gas company and one of the largest investor-owned energy companies in the world. It is the largest utility in the UK, and second largest in the US.

It owns the high-voltage electricity transmission network in England and Wales and operates the system across Great Britain. It also owns and operates the high-pressure gas transmission system in Britain, and the distribution business delivers gas to 11 million homes and businesses.

National Grid is investing billions of pounds in the nation's infrastructure, providing safe and secure energy supplies, which is vital to communities. It is committed to safeguarding our global environment for future generations and providing all customers with the highest standards of service through investment in the networks.

Operating safe and reliable transmission and distribution networks requires continuous maintenance of the existing

network of overhead lines, cables and pipelines. The network passes through a variety of landscapes and habitats, including areas designated for their conservation value. In preparation for work, National Grid seeks the advice of relevant experts to minimise as far as practicable any impacts these activities could have on species and their habitats through careful planning and mitigation measures.

National Grid has maintained a close relationship with The Tree Council since the early 1990s, and has sponsored The Tree Council's Tree Warden Scheme for over 10 years. In addition to supporting the Tree Warden Scheme, National Grid also has a network of environmental education centres across the UK, all sited on land owned by the company adjacent to electricity substations. They are centres of excellence for environmental education and have been developed with local authorities and environmental charities, demonstrating how industry and the environment can develop strong partnerships to the benefit of all.

An important part of National Grid's infrastructure maintenance programme is to manage the growth of trees near equipment (high-voltage overhead lines, underground cables and pipelines), helping to protect the public and the network by maintaining statutory safety clearances. National Grid has planted thousands of trees to screen equipment and reduce its visible impact.

Along with the centres, sponsorship of the Tree Warden Scheme helps to minimise the environmental impacts associated with National Grid's operational activities. However, as most of National Grid's assets are sited on land owned by other people, such as grantors, effective tree management can be difficult to achieve.

Sponsorship of the Tree Warden Scheme has helped National Grid to build and maintain positive relationships with local authorities and to raise its profile among other stakeholder groups, such as planners, ministers, MPs and environmental groups.

The development of National Grid's vegetation and tree management policy has been fundamental in ensuring that when planning new transmission work, it seeks to avoid loss of mature trees and ancient woodland habitats. Where this is unavoidable, it aims to plant four trees for every mature tree removed as a result of its operations.

The Tree Bank, a process developed in conjunction with The Tree Council, helps to deliver the objectives of the vegetation and tree management policy.

The environmental management plan for each of National Grid's projects identifies how many trees and hedges are to be felled or removed along the work route. The hedges are reinstated as before for practical, ecological and agricultural reasons. Some trees are reinstated at the request of the landowner, and others will be used to screen new or existing assets, such as substations.

The remaining trees are then valued at a figure agreed between The Tree Council and National Grid, and the resulting funds are placed into the Tree Bank. The funds are then transferred to The Tree Council as a grant to deliver the required number of trees in the specified geographical area.

Local Tree Wardens and their coordinators will then identify any opportunities to enhance woodland, amenity treescape and hedgerow biodiversity within the local community, and will work in partnership with The Tree Council to plant the trees.

With expert advice from The Tree Council, and the help of its army of local volunteers, National Grid works hard to manage trees in a safe and sustainable way.

Twenty questions

Well, a couple of dozen of them, actually. But they'll help you get to grips with what a tree is all about.

What is a tree?

Although this appears to be a simple question, it is in fact quite complicated. Simplistically, a tree is a large woody organism. That definition, however, is inadequate – for example, in the case of small willows, which are small woody organisms, yet can be described as trees. Another definition is that a tree is any plant that has a self-supporting perennial (ie living more than one year) woody stem. This definition works better than the previous one, except when considering the distinction between a tree and a shrub.

Some tree books have created the distinction that a tree has a single trunk and an elevated head of branches, whereas a shrub branches from the base, with no obvious trunk. Unfortunately, the way a tree is managed can thus make it a shrub; or a shrub that has not been cut can become a tree.

Interestingly, in Tree Preservation Order (TPO) legislation the term 'tree' is not defined. Indeed, for the purposes of the TPO legislation, the High Court has held that a tree is 'anything which ordinarily one would call a tree'.

In this book we have used the definition that 'a tree is regarded as a plant that has a self-supporting perennial woody stem', which covers everything from a tiny dwarf willow to a towering giant redwood, and we don't worry about the distinction between shrubs and trees.

What is a broadleaf?

The broadleaf trees are angiosperms – plants with their seeds hidden inside a fruit. Angiosperm trees can be of two types: one produces two leaves (or more) from the seeds (dicotyledons) – eg oaks and birches; the other produces a single leaf from the seed (monocotyledons) – eg palms, aloes and yuccas. Most of the world's trees are broadleaf.

What is a conifer?

Conifers are usually thought of as trees that bear cones. However, they are actually gymnosperms – plants that have 'naked' seeds that can be seen in the cone or the fruit without having to cut it open. There are approximately 650 species of conifer around the world, which include yew and juniper. There are also many hundreds of subspecies and varieties in cultivation.

What is the difference between evergreen and deciduous?

An evergreen tree is a plant that retains green leaves all year round. A deciduous tree loses its leaves completely for part of the year, becoming bare and leafless. The terms 'evergreen' and 'deciduous' are sometimes taken as shorthand for conifers (evergreen) and broadleaves (deciduous). However, this does not work in every case as there are deciduous conifers, for example dawn redwood and larch, and evergreen broadleaf trees, including holly.

How many tree species are there in the world?

It is thought that there are between 80,000 and 100,000 tree species in the world, the difference being a reflection of the difficulty of defining a 'tree'.

Of the world's tree flora, nearly nine per cent (7,388 species) are documented as being globally threatened with extinction, while more than 90 tree species have already become extinct.

What is wood?

Wood is formed as a result of the growth of a tree. It is a hard, fibrous, substance, which occurs under the tree's bark. As a tree grows, its stem is formed of five main layers. The inner two layers are the wood – the inner heartwood and the outer sapwood.

Sapwood conducts water around the tree.

Heartwood (where it is present, for it is not found in all trees) is the material usually sought for timber.

What are tree rings?

Trees grow outwards by the addition of new wood immediately under the bark. As the tree grows, it creates visible growth rings, which in some species have a light and dark band within them. The differences in the widths of the rings are due to changes in growth rate from year to year. The rings can be counted to determine the age of the tree, and used to date wood taken from trees in the past: this practice is known as dendrochronology.

What are leaves for?

Leaves are the elements of the plant specially designed for photosynthesis. Leaf cells contain discrete structures called chloroplasts, which convert the energy of sunlight into chemical energy to produce sugars. The full photosynthetic reactions are complex, but they are usually simplified as:

Carbon dioxide + Water + Light energy

$\downarrow$

in the presence of Chlorophyll

$\downarrow$

Glucose (sugar) + Oxygen + Water

The plant takes in carbon dioxide to produce sugars for itself and, as a waste product, emits oxygen into the atmosphere.

Why are leaves green?

Leaves are normally green in colour as a result of
chlorophyll from which the tree produces its food. This
amazing compound uses the red and blue light in sunlight
to produce the chemical reactions needed to turn carbon
dioxide and water into sugars and oxygen, resulting in the
green light being reflected and giving the leaf its colour.

How many leaves does a tree have?

A mature English oak
(*Quercus robur*) has
approximately 700,000
leaves, while an American
elm (*Ulmus americana*)
has as many as five million.
Conversely, a large apple tree
may have only about 50,000.

How do leaves fall off in the autumn?

With deciduous trees, the mechanism to shed leaves is called abscission. Leaf fall is not a random process, but is a deliberate sequence, triggered by decreasing daylight and reduced air temperature. Across the base of the leaf is the abscission zone, which breaks as the autumn approaches, allowing the leaf to fall from the tree. The breaking of this zone is caused by increased levels of the plant hormones ethylene, abscisic acid and/or auxin. A leaf scar remains on the twig at the site of the shed leaf.

Although leaves grow to a finite size in one season, the twigs they grow on continue to expand into branches year on year, so in due course all leaves, even needles, are forced to drop off.

Why do leaves fall off in the autumn?

Simply to save the tree from storm damage by reducing its resistance to wind, ice and snow. Shedding leaves also reduces water loss at a time when replacement soil moisture is limited by low temperatures.

How much water do trees use?

Trees lose water by a process called transpiration. An apple tree 2m high may use up to 700 litres of water in a summer. A fully grown birch tree may use 17,000 litres, while a large oak may use up to 40,000 litres. An Olympic-sized swimming pool contains approximately 3,125,000 litres of water – or enough to keep nearly 80 oak trees going for a summer.

Do I need to water young trees?

Young, newly planted trees have limited root systems that cannot withstand long periods without adequate soil moisture. Trees that have been in the ground for only a year or two are at greatest risk, but if dry weather continues for long periods, then older trees may also begin to suffer. Signs of drought stress can vary from tree to tree, the most common symptom being wilting of the leaves, leading to browning and drying of the entire leaf. The key to successful tree watering is to soak the root system deeply and not to reapply water until the soil starts to dry out. Avoid frequent light applications as this can cause surface rooting and lead to overwatering. Young trees – those that have been in the ground for a year or two – should be well soaked once every seven to 10 days. Older, more established trees should be deeply watered every two weeks or so.

What are roots for?

The basic functions of roots
are to allow trees to take up
water, to take in mineral
nutrients, to move the water
and minerals to the tree's trunk
and to provide support and
anchorage to the tree. Roots
also store starch and oils for
the tree to use when growing,
and produce a range of
plant hormones.

How deep do roots go and how far do they spread?

Most trees begin life with a taproot emerging from the
seed. This goes straight down into the soil (if possible)
then, after a few years, side roots develop to create a
wide-spreading fibrous root system, with mainly horizontal
surface roots and only a few vertical deep roots. A typical
mature tree – 30-50m tall – has a root system that may
extend horizontally in all directions, frequently as far as
the tree is tall, but with over 90 per cent of the roots in
the top 1m of soil. Recent research also suggests that
roots can sometimes extend out far beyond the drip line
of the canopy. Research at Kew Gardens showed that none
of the trees studied (nearly 700 in total, of 36 species)
had roots which reached deeper than 3m into the soil.
Although some trees can have deeper roots, a depth of
less than 3m is the norm.

What is bark for?

Bark is the outermost layer of a tree. It overlays the wood and is made up of the inner phloem, which carries sugar around the tree, and the outer bark, which acts like a waterproof skin. Part of the outer bark layer is filled with air, tannin and/or waxy substances and is called the phelloderm layer. The purpose of the phelloderm is to provide protection against damage, pests and diseases, as well as dehydration and extreme temperatures. In some trees the phelloderm layer has become substantially thicker, to protect the tree from fire or dehydration (eg cork oak and giant redwood).

Which is currently the world's tallest tree?

During the summer of 2006, researchers from the Humboldt State University discovered the tallest recorded tree in the world, a coast redwood which they named Hyperion. This tree is 115.5m tall, beating the previous record holder – the 112.9m-tall Stratosphere Giant.

The researchers were exploring rugged areas of the Redwood National and State Parks in the USA and also found two other redwoods taller than the Stratosphere Giant. This suggests that there may have been many other massive redwoods before the commercial logging of the area, which stopped in 1978.

Which is the world's rarest tree?

There are several trees of which only one known specimen exists in the world, including the café marron from the island of Rodrigues and the *Pennantia baylisiana* on Great Island in the Three Kings Islands Group, New Zealand.

Which tree has the greatest recorded girth?

It's a sweet chestnut, which is known as 'The Tree of a Hundred Horses', and it can be found growing on Linguaglossa Road in Sant'Alfio, on the eastern slope of Mount Etna in Sicily.

The tree had a circumference of 57.9m when measured in 1780. It has now split into three parts.

EDWARD PARKER / ALAMY

Which is the oldest living individual tree?

The oldest living individual tree is said to be a bristlecone pine, nicknamed 'Methuselah' (after the longest-lived person in the Bible). The tree, which stands in the Bristlecone Pine Forest in the White Mountains of eastern California, was found by Dr Edmund Schulman (USA) in 1957, who estimated it to be 4,600 years old.

What percentage of Britain is covered in trees and how does this compare with the rest of Europe?

The Countryside Surveys of Great Britain and Northern Ireland estimate that woodland covers nearly 12 per cent of the UK. By comparison, 28 per cent of France is wooded, 29 per cent of Spain, 30 per cent of Germany and 33 per cent of Italy and Greece. Indeed, in Europe, only Ireland and Iceland have a lower woodland cover than Britain. Along with the woodland cover, the UK also still has many trees remaining as in-field trees, especially in parklands and wood pastures and in our extensive hedgerow network, plus many trees in our parks and gardens.

How many trees are there in Britain?

There are an estimated four billion trees in Britain including those in woods and forests. The number of trees growing outside woodland is estimated at 123 million.

Which British tree supports most insect life?

Research by Oxford University in conjunction with the Biological Records Centre at Monks Wood has resulted in published league tables for the numbers of different insect species living on the leaves of particular tree species throughout Britain. These suggest that willow supports the most, with 450 species, but these occur on five willow species. Oak supports 423 on two species – pedunculate and sessile. The top score for the number of different species on a single tree is hawthorn, with 209.

These data should not be regarded as the final word, since new finds on all species of tree are constantly being reported. A lot depends on the ecosystem: for example, a tree in mixed woodland is likely to support more insects than one in isolation. In some areas, however, atmospheric pollution is taking its toll on micro-organisms, so numbers are severely reduced. Interestingly, some exotic trees are finding favour with British insects: in Wales, for example, southern beech is home to many insects that are more usually found on oak.

Taking trees as a whole, rather than just those supporting leaf-eating insects, the picture is somewhat different. The wood decay insects and those associated with leaf litter, blossom, and fruits and seeds are also important. Sycamore is extremely valuable for wildlife biomass because it supports a superabundance of aphids on which aphid feeders can feast.

It's as easy as one, two, tree

There's nothing easier than growing your own trees. You don't need green fingers or a licence – just plenty of enthusiasm.

Children: they'll love growing trees, too

The great thing about growing trees from seed is that it is something everyone can do. No special equipment is required as seeds can be planted directly in the ground if you have the space or, if space is limited, they can be germinated and grown on in recycled cartons and plastic pots, using compost or garden soil, on an outside window sill.

Some seeds require treatment before they are planted but, again, this requires no special equipment. If they do need stratifying (which means keeping them cold before planting) then putting them in the fridge in a plastic bag works well.

Once you have got the bug and germinated and grown a tree from seed, you will find that every time you go on a walk you will be looking out for trees with seeds and fruits to harvest. Again, you won't need any special equipment for this – just have a paper bag and a pencil in your pocket.

Growing trees from seed is also a great activity to do with children. The Tree Council's Seed Gathering Season provides a good focus for this (see page 10). You don't have to worry too much about where they will be planted, as the magic of seeing something grow is what is important. Seeds like horse chestnuts, acorns and sycamore keys, which are large and germinate reliably, are perfect for small fingers to plant without damage. If you then don't have the space for these large trees, they will grow in pots for a few years before you have to recycle them.

There are lots of reasons to grow trees from seed:

■ To grow trees that thrive locally.

■ To increase the numbers of rare native species.

■ To produce lots of trees cheaply.

■ To grow a specific tree that may be difficult to find at the garden centre.

The most important thing to remember is that most trees are easy to grow from seed, so if in doubt give it a go and see what happens. If a tree is difficult to grow from seed or requires specific treatment you'll discover what to do in the pages ahead.

What to grow

If you are going to go to the trouble of growing your own trees, then you'll want to grow the right ones.

Growing the right tree for the right place is very important. How many times do you see front gardens with massive trees in them that were probably planted as small trees by people who didn't realise how big they were going to get? Sometimes they're there because they've been grown from seed by previous occupants – horse chestnuts, for instance, are very easy to grow and, when a few years old, make small trees with beautiful characteristic hand-shaped leaves that are attractive to children. But, if left for a few more years, these fast-growing trees can become too big for a small front garden, with their heavy canopy that can shade windows and cut out light.

There are other things to consider apart from size and speed of growth when deciding what trees to grow.

A little help from friends

City farms, community gardens, allotment groups, local schools and park 'friends' groups may all be able to help find places to plant trees. And remember, your local Tree Warden is an invaluable person to offer advice. You can contact yours through the local coordinator, who is usually the tree officer at your local council. Bear in mind that not all sites are suitable for trees. If there are none where you are thinking of planting it may be for a very good reason – it may be a habitat such as moorland or marsh, which would be damaged by tree planting.

If space is limited and you only have room for a small tree, look for something that has interest for more than one season. Try to pick a tree that has attractive flowers and good autumn colour as well as an interesting winter silhouette or bark. In small spaces, also go for trees with a fastigiate shape (ie its branches are upright and close together), or ones that can be easily pruned and maintained as small trees.

If you have a larger garden with space for more than one tree don't make the mistake of planting specimen trees too close together. Look at the size and spread they are likely to achieve in 20 years and give them room, or you may be faced with the choice of which tree to remove later on. Alternatively, if you are planting a grove of trees or a shelter belt, you can deliberately overplant and remove selected trees as they become too crowded, leaving the best and strongest ones standing.

If you are wanting to encourage wildlife into your garden, go for native species or ornamental trees which have fleshy fruits that will be attractive to birds.

If you are growing trees to increase the numbers of a rare species in your area, contact your region's Wildlife Trust or local authority conservation officer.

If you are still not sure what you want to grow, look at what does well in the rest of your neighbourhood, particularly if you live near the coast or in exposed areas where trees will need to be adapted to a very specific climate.

Some trees will live for a while in large tubs and pots, but all thrive best when planted out into a suitable site. Be ruthless and only plant out well-grown seedlings.

Finally, if you are thinking of planting trees anywhere that you don't own, you need to seek the owner's permission.

Collect your seeds

In the UK most trees fruit throughout the autumn – the exact time is dependent on the weather and the species of tree. Seeds may be viable well into the winter and most, in fact, are programmed not to germinate until the spring. Provided they haven't rotted or been eaten by wildlife, they stand a good chance of germinating and growing into a tree if picked at the end of the year. This means that seeds of one form or another can be gathered throughout the autumn and winter.

Few trees fruit every year, and good crops are intermittent. The process of growing young trees therefore begins by keeping an eye on the quantities of fruits developing. This means that, when you are starting, it's best to be

Handy hints

■ Always leave some seeds behind – they are an important food source for wildlife.

■ Avoid collecting in wet weather when the seeds are wet (unless you are going to plant straight away) as they will not store well.

■ Use paper bags to take your seeds home. Don't use plastic bags as they may cause the seeds to become too moist, reducing their chance of germination.

■ Collect seeds from healthy, well-grown trees. If the tree you want to collect seeds from is on private land it is very important to ask the permission of the tree's owner.

■ If you are collecting from tall trees where the seeds are well above reach, don't try to climb up to get them as this could be dangerous. Instead, look for fallen seeds on the ground.

■ As you are collecting, put seeds in different bags and label them. If you come across a tree you don't recognise make a note on the bag of any distinguishing features and put a leaf in to help later identification.

flexible about what you collect and grow. If the tree you were hoping to grow hasn't fruited, use this book to find trees with similar characteristics.

Check that the fruits are ripe. There is more information about how to tell when seeds are ready to collect for each species in this book's tree descriptions.

When ripe, the fruits should be picked directly from the tree, or gathered from the ground when freshly fallen. It is worth bearing in mind that some tree seeds are poisonous. The commonest of these are the yew and laburnum, but there are others. If you are collecting with children, and unsure, it is best to play it safe and make sure you and they eat no seeds at all.

Seed preparation

Got your seeds? So, which bits do you actually need? And then what do you do with them? The answers are simple…

Seeds need different forms of preparation before sowing, depending on the type. These can broadly be broken down into five categories:

- ◾ Pods (eg Indian bean tree and laburnum)
- ◾ Winged seeds (eg ash and silver birch)
- ◾ Nuts (eg hazel and oak)
- ◾ Fleshy fruits (eg elder and crab apple)
- ◾ Cones (eg pine and alder).

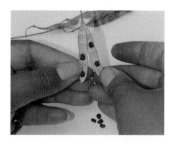

Pods

Simply break open and strip out the seeds.

Winged seeds

If in pairs break in half.

Nuts

These should be put in a bowl of water – the ones that float are generally not viable and should be discarded.

Fleshy fruits

Remove the flesh by cutting the fruit in half to reveal the seeds or, if they are small, mash them in water, put the resulting pulp in a sieve and rinse under running water.

Cones

Put in a paper bag and leave until the cone has opened, then shake and the seeds will be caught in the bag.

Stratifying, or the art of keeping cool

Most tree seeds require stratifying to germinate. The basic technique is to try and simulate a cold winter, as the seed is programmed to germinate in the spring as the temperature rises.

With small seeds, the easiest way to do this is to soak them in cold water for 24 hours and then put them in a plastic bag in the bottom of the fridge (clearly labelled) for a couple of months.

If you have a large quantity of seeds, or bigger ones, stratify them outside. Do this by mixing the seeds into moist compost, then put the mixture in a covered bucket and leave outside all winter. Cover the top with wire netting to stop mice and squirrels eating the seeds.

And now, it's time to sow

Once collected, prepared and stratified, seeds can be sown into containers or directly into the ground – either into a seedbed or the site where they are to grow.

Sowing into containers

Almost any container that will hold soil or compost will do for growing trees, so this is an ideal opportunity to recycle. If soil is unavailable, use a peat-free or loam-based compost. Ideal containers include:

■ the waxed card cartons that fruit juice comes in. The advantage of using these is that the whole thing can be planted out so that the seedlings' roots don't get disturbed during planting

■ large yogurt pots – make a hole in the bottom

■ plastic milk bottles – cut the top off and make a hole in the bottom.

It's as easy as...

■ Larger seeds can be sown individually. Make a small hole in the compost with the end of a pencil or your finger, drop the seed in and cover. The seed should have roughly its own depth of compost above it.

■ Sow small seeds, a pinch at a time, onto the surface of the compost and cover with a sprinkle of sharp sand or compost. Once the seeds have germinated, gently pull out the weaker smaller seedlings, leaving one good seedling in each pot.

■ Once you have sown your seeds, put them outside in a sheltered spot out of direct sunlight and strong wind. Large seeds and nuts will need protection from rodents, so cover them with netting – the netting bags from oranges are good for this. Remove the netting once the seeds have germinated.

■ The compost should be kept moist but not waterlogged, or the seedling will rot. Seedlings may be potted into larger containers and grown on or planted out once their roots have filled the container.

When to pot out

To see if a seedling requires either planting out or potting on, put your hand over the compost surface to support the seedling and gently turn the pot upside down. Tap and remove the root ball from the pot. If the roots are starting to fill the pot, spiralling round the inside, then the seedling is ready.

Do you always need to sow into pots?

Seeds can also be sown directly into the ground – this is a good method if you have the space. Mark out the seedbed and prepare as you would for any seeds, dig over and remove all weeds. If the soil is heavy, dig in course grit or sharp sand to make the seedbed free draining. Plant large seeds individually, using a pencil or a finger to make holes at regular intervals. For small seeds, create a shallow furrow in the soil into which you sow the seeds, and thin once they have germinated.

You can protect seeds in a seedbed with a wire fence. The seedlings will need watering in dry weather and can be planted out once they are large enough to handle in the following autumn.

When seeds aren't the answer

Sowing seeds isn't the only way of creating new trees. Taking cuttings is a way to propagate species that don't produce viable seed or that don't grow true from seed.

Hardwood cuttings

Trees suitable for propagation from hardwood cuttings include willow, alder, plane, poplar, mulberry, dogwood and fig.

Hardwood cuttings are taken in winter when the tree is dormant.

It's as easy as...

■ Cut strong vigorous shoots from this year's growth.

■ Using a spade, cut a trench in the soil – choose a sheltered spot out of direct sunlight.

■ Insert the cuttings, being careful to keep them the right way up. For some trees with small buds it's easy to get this wrong – one way of helping is to do a straight cut at the bottom of the cutting and a slanted one at the top when preparing them.

■ Firm them in, being careful not to damage the buds.

■ For multi-stemmed trees, leave about 30-50cm of stem, with several buds, above the soil surface.

■ For single-stemmed trees the top of the cutting should be just below the soil surface.

Lift the cutting in the following autumn, once the leaves have fallen. For small cuttings use a trowel, being careful to get as much of the root ball as possible. For larger cuttings use a spade and cut around the root ball. Only lift when you are ready to pot on or plant out.

Semi-ripe cuttings

Variegated trees that don't come true from seeds and evergreens, such as holly, box and many conifers, can be propagated using semi-ripe cuttings. These are taken towards the end of summer from this season's growth.

■ Cut 5-20cm pieces of stem, depending on the size of the plant.

■ Strip the leaves off the cuttings, leaving about three leaves at the tip of each one.

■ Trim the remaining leaves, if they are large, to reduce water loss.

■ Trim the bottom ends just below a leaf joint and dip in rooting powder.

■ Insert five or six cuttings around the edge of a 10cm pot, or large yogurt pot, of gritty free-draining compost. Remember to make a hole in the bottom for drainage.

■ Cover with a plastic bag or put in a propagator.

Once they have rooted, pot the cuttings into individual pots and harden off outside in a sheltered spot.

Softwood cuttings

Softwood cuttings are taken from the tree at the height of the growing season, in late spring/early summer. Suitable trees for softwood cuttings are ornamental cherries – the tip of the growing shoot is used.

Softwood cuttings root quickly – once rooted, carefully lift and plant out into individual pots.

It's as easy as...

■ Trim cuttings to 5-10cm below a leaf joint, and remove the bottom leaves. Dip the cut end in rooting powder.

■ Insert into a pot or seed tray filled with free-draining compost.

■ Cover with a plastic bag and put on a window sill or in a propagator out of sunlight.

Root cuttings

Traditionally, many trees were propagated using root cuttings. A spade would be used to cut through the roots, and the cut root would then throw up shoots or suckers. These would then be used to produce new trees. Elms were propagated widely in this way because they don't produce reliable seeds.

Root cuttings are worth considering for the following trees: elm, willow and aspen.

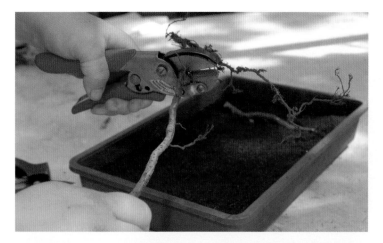

It's as easy as...

■ Choose a healthy tree.

■ Take root cuttings in January and February, when the soil isn't frozen but before the tree has started into growth.

■ Dig into the soil and use a knife to remove sections of root that are about pencil thickness.

■ Carefully replace the soil and firm down with your foot.

■ Cut the roots into manageable sections that will fit into a seed tray or box without touching, and cover with soil or compost. Keep damp.

■ Leave in a cold frame or cover with plastic and put in a sheltered position until the roots produce shoots.

■ Once these have sprouted, cut off the shoots at soil level and pot up using a rooting powder, as for softwood cuttings.

Once the roots have started to shoot – and have at least three sets of leaves – they are ready to pot on. Keep cutting shoots until the roots are exhausted.

Layering

This is a method of propagation that mimics nature – many trees and shrubs do this naturally when their branches touch the ground and for this reason this method is more commonly used to propagate shrubs with branches that sweep the ground. Suitable trees are the evergreen and deciduous magnolias.

It's as easy as...

◼ In early spring, take a vigorous pliant branch.

◼ Bend it down so that last season's growth touches the soil.

◼ Where it touches the soil cut a small notch in the bark.

◼ Scrape a shallow trench in the ground.

◼ Pin the branch down onto the soil with a bent piece of wire – cut-up coat hangers are good for this.

◼ Cover with soil.

The branch will root and be ready to be separated from its parent by the following spring.

Grafting

This is difficult for the amateur but is used commercially to produce both ornamental and fruit trees. It is used because:

◼ the tree matures more quickly, as the graft material is being joined to an established root system

◼ the type of rootstock used will influence the habit of the tree, so it is possible to produce trees of different sizes.

The basic principle is to join the graft material, or scion, from one tree with the rootstock from another – usually of the same species – to make a new tree. Both are cut and the two surfaces bound together until they fuse and become one.

Planting out trees

Just as with children, one day a young tree will outgrow its first home. The trick is knowing when it's time for them to move on.

When to plant

It is best to grow the tree seedlings or cuttings on in a sheltered seedbed or in containers until they are big enough to handle easily. This will depend on the species, but you can usually leave them there for up to two years. If they are growing in containers, make sure they don't get pot bound. It's easy to check for this – once roots start to appear out of the holes in the bottom of the container it's time to pot on into a larger size.

The smaller trees are when they are planted out into their final position the better, as their roots are less likely to be damaged and they will establish faster.

Bare-root trees (seedlings that have been grown in open ground) can be transplanted and planted into their final position any time from November to March.

Container-grown trees can be planted all year round. In all cases, avoid days when the ground is frozen. A good time to plant is during The Tree Council's National Tree Week, from late November until the first weekend in December.

Deciduous trees are best planted before Christmas. They are less likely to suffer from drought if planted in the autumn or early winter. Evergreen trees are best planted either early or late in the planting season. Spring planting should not take place until the soil has begun to warm and the first flush of new growth occurs.

It's as easy as...

■ Dig a hole big enough to accommodate the root ball.

■ Break up the soil at the bottom of the hole.

■ If using a stake, drive it into the hole.

■ Put the tree into the hole and backfill, keeping the level of the soil around the trunk the same as it was before it was transplanted.

■ If using a stake, tie it to the tree trunk using a tree tie.

■ If using a tree guard, slide it over the branches, being careful not to cause any damage, and secure in place with a stake or cane.

■ Clear any weeds from around the tree, and mulch.

In dry areas, late autumn planting is best for most species, as this gives trees a chance to become established before spring droughts. In wet areas, early spring planting is best.

Ideally, the site should be drained of excess water. Where soils are wet and then freeze there is a risk of 'frost lift', which can devastate newly planted trees, though this is unlikely in most years.

Although container-grown trees can be planted at any time of year, these guidelines will give the best results for them too. If planting is in late spring or summer, container-grown trees should be watered during dry spells for the first growing season.

Ideally, trees should be lifted, transported and replanted without interruption, as a tree's fine roots can die if they dry out, which will mean that the tree will not establish well or may die soon after it is planted.

Stakes, guards and shelters

Trees, especially when young, are extremely vulnerable to damage from both animals and people so, depending on their situation, may need protection.

Larger transplanted trees can also be susceptible to damage from the wind, so may need staking.

Points to consider

■ Cost
Protective measures can add considerably to initial costs. It is usually cheaper to protect groups rather than individual trees.

■ Maintenance
All forms of protection add to maintenance.

■ Appearance
Protection can sometimes be unsightly.

■ Susceptibility
Is the species of tree susceptible to animal damage? Is there a more resistant choice of species?

■ Site
Is there a strong prevailing wind? Is there a problem in the area with a particular animal?

Aftercare

So now you have your tree. You weren't thinking of abandoning it, though, were you? Just like humans, trees benefit from TLC throughout their life – and it's a simple and enjoyable process.

The first five years

Care for trees in their first five years is vital. Many young trees die from neglect, especially from a lack of basic weed control. It is important to check on newly planted trees at least once a year and carry out a few simple maintenance tasks, including:

- watering (if necessary)
- clearing grass and weeds
- adjusting/replacing/removing tree stakes and ties
- checking guards and shelters
- ensuring roots remain covered
- pruning carefully (if required).

It's as easy as...

Watering

- Except in long dry spells, it is rarely necessary to water transplants, provided they were planted at the right time of year (in the winter when they are dormant and the ground is wet), with the roots kept moist, and attention is paid to weeding and mulching. This is important both at the time of planting and in the first few years after that.

- If watering is required, give the tree a very thorough soaking – about 50-75 litres per square metre each week in dry weather, during the growing season. Watering 'little and often' will only encourage surface rooting, increasing the tree's vulnerability to drought and scorching by the sun.

Clearing grass and weeds

Grasses and other fast-growing, leafy perennials compete with young trees for moisture, nutrients, space and light. To help the tree get established, it is important to keep an area of about a square metre around it free of weeds for at least three years.

It's as easy as...

Weeding

■ If hand weeding, be careful not to disturb surface roots.

■ Pull up grasses, woody shrubs and large-leaved herbaceous plants so that they are uprooted. They should not be cut back or mown, as this encourages growth. Hoeing can damage the roots.

Weed control – mulching

Mulching is a simple and effective way of controlling weeds and it also:

■ keeps the ground moist and cool

■ means there is no need to use lawnmowers or strimmers near the tree, risking damage to the bark, which could kill the tree

■ avoids using chemicals.

Organic mulches also gradually improve the soil as they decompose, particularly if it is compacted or eroded.

Mulches are especially useful. They should be applied immediately after planting, but not until any weeds have been pulled up and the tree has been watered. One application is usually adequate, but trees benefit from mulching in later years if there is little natural plant litter.

Loose organic mulches include:

■ leaf litter

■ spoiled hay (available from farms)

■ well-rotted manure

■ well-rotted lawn clippings

■ composted bark

■ wood chips.

Why pruning is the plum choice

Careful pruning of young trees can prevent problems in later life, but bad pruning can kill trees or make them hazardous, so training is important.

As well as pruning to remove dead or diseased twigs or branches, formative pruning is important to produce a strong lead shoot. With transplants and seedlings this should be carried out when the tree has developed sufficiently, sometime after its second year.

It is not necessary to apply wound paint or dressing. Research shows that they do not reduce decay or make the tree heal more quickly, and they rarely prevent disease.

No work should be carried out during the breeding season if, for example, there is any risk of disturbing nesting birds. Tree seedlings can gradually be pruned to form a standard, a process which sometimes also occurs naturally. This 'feathering' channels food to the main stem, which becomes thicker and stronger.

It's as easy as...

Pruning

■ Use a sharp pair of secateurs or, for thicker branches, a pruning saw.

■ Remove any dead, diseased or damaged wood.

■ Cut out weak or crossing branches, while maintaining the tree's natural form.

■ Decide which branches to prune back or remove before you start.

■ Never cut flush with the stem or trunk – always outside the branch collar (the slight swelling on the branch where it joins the trunk) – to avoid damaging the tree's natural protective zone.

Year 1

■ Remove any weak or competing leaders.

■ On the lowest third of the tree, cut back laterals to the main stem.

■ On the middle third, cut back laterals by half.

Years 2 and 3

■ Repeat the procedure until the tree has about 1.8m of clear stem.

For the real experts (you're halfway to being one)

If you really get into the whole business of tree growing and maintenance, then there's an exciting new world that will open up for you.

Other tree management techniques

There are various ways of managing trees – some for aesthetic reasons and others more for economic and safety reasons. As with any kind of surgery on a mature tree requiring a chainsaw, this is something for experts to carry out, but it is important to understand the techniques so that you know what needs to be done.

Coppicing

■ Coppicing is the regular pruning of a tree close to the ground so that many new strong shoots grow from the base. It is done in late winter or early spring.

■ Cut back all stems to the base, leaving the swollen basal wood unpruned.

Pollarding

■ Pollarding involves pruning a tree back to its main stem or branch framework, stimulating new shoots above the height where animals can graze.

■ You should seek expert advice in the management of ancient pollards. However, coppicing or pollarding young trees or managing traditionally coppiced woods are practical activities that many community groups undertake.

■ Managing pollards is best carried out by a tree surgeon who has specialist experience of this. The basic technique is to cut back the branches every few years when the tree is dormant.

Coppicing and pollarding are two management techniques which were traditionally practised to give a regular supply of firewood, timber or pliable stems for basketwork and fencing. Today, pollarded trees and coppiced woodlands are particularly important for their wildlife value and as landscape features. Pollarding is also still used to restrict the size of street trees.

Later life

If you love your tree, you'll keep coming back to it as the years roll by. These are ways in which experts can help you.

Crown thinning

Crown thinning involves removing selected branches within the tree canopy to allow more light to penetrate through and reduce the wind resistance of the tree. It does not affect the height or the shape of the tree.

Trees may be thinned by up to 30 per cent – one branch in three.

Dead wood and crossing branches should be pruned out as a priority as the tree is thinned.

Crown lifting

Removing a tree's lower branches can be done to allow access, clearance for buildings, vehicles or pedestrians, or to open the view beneath the canopy.

Crown reduction

The aim of crown reduction is to reduce the height and spread of a tree, while retaining its natural shape. This allows more light to pass over and around a tree. It also helps to create the statutory clearance that is required for power and telephone lines. Not all types of tree respond well to this treatment.

The leaves consist of three-lobed leaflets, rather like a clover leaf. The fruit has brown 'pea-like' pods containing black poisonous seeds

Laburnum

Laburnum anagyroides

A small deciduous tree or large shrub, laburnum seldom exceeds 9m in height. This tree is in the same botanical order as the pea family, which explains its yellow hanging 'pea' flowers and three-leaflet leaves. Laburnum grows well on most soils, provided they are not overdry. It requires a sunny position, and does well in sandy soils.

Introduced to Britain in 1596 by the famous gardener and plant collector Tradescant, it can now be found growing widely throughout the country.

Unfortunately, for such a widely grown tree, its seeds are poisonous and contain a highly toxic alkaloid – cytisine. Cytisine's side effects can include nausea and, in larger doses, even death via respiratory failure. One report showed that 10 seeds were fatal to a child.

The heartwood of laburnum gets darker when exposed to light, becoming chocolate brown. This rich colour, combined with its wide use by cabinetmakers, made it in 1812 'the most valuable timber grown in Scotland'.

9m (mature)
6m (10 years)
2m (5 years)

Seed guide

The brown seed pods are about 5cm long, and split to reveal small black poisonous seeds. Collect the ripe pods in September/October before they split open. In March, puncture the hard, water-impermeable seed coat with a file or knife – without damaging the embryo within; alternatively cover the seeds in about five times their volume of boiling water and allow to cool for 12 hours. Sow chipped or swollen seeds in an outdoor seedbed in March or April.

Did you know?

Oddly for a poisonous plant, laburnum was widely used for hedging in Ceredigion, as well as Carmarthenshire, in Wales. (See, for example, the A487 between Llanarth and Cardigan.)

The dark glossy leaves have smaller teeth than crab apples, with a longer leaf stalk. The small green pears ripen and contain brown seeds

Wild Pear

Pyrus communis

The wild pear can be found scattered alongside road verges, in hedgerows and on woodland edges throughout Britain. It is also planted in parks and gardens. It is an uncommon tree, and may actually be rare, as many supposed wild pears are actually 'wildings' – trees descended from domesticated pears. The wild tree has spiny branches and produces small gritty pears. The dark brown bark also cracks into distinctive plates.

The pale pink wood takes stain easily and was used for veneers, woodturning, carving and for making musical instruments, including flutes and – when stained – black piano keys.

The flowers of the wild pear attract insects in the spring, although to the human nose they smell fishy. The tree also provides excellent growing conditions for mistletoe.

15m (mature)
9m (10 years)
3m (5 years)

Seed guide

Collect the fruit from the tree or the ground when ripe. Cut open the pear, and if the seeds are brown this confirms that they are ripe. Carefully remove the seeds and stratify them, usually for one winter. In cool autumns, germination can be improved by keeping stratifying seeds at room temperature for two weeks, before putting them outside for the winter. Select and sow germinating seeds in spring.

Did you know?

Another pear species grows in Plymouth. Called the Plymouth pear (*Pyrus cordata*), it is protected under Schedule 8 of the Wildlife and Countryside Act 1981 and is the only tree protected because of its rarity. It is also listed in the British Red Data Book of Endangered Species.

And now... the trees

On the following pages there are 66 species of tree. You'll find specific seed guides and a silhouette of each tree, which gives an idea of the relative heights it will reach after five years, 10 years and at maturity. These height figures are for guidance only, as tree growth is dependent on many conditions.

35m (mature)

16m (10 years)

4m (5 years)

Size matters

You'll notice that the list begins with guelder rose and ends with European lime. That means it's not alphabetical, nor does it follow any botanical order. In fact, we've simply ordered the trees based on the space needed to grow them.

Basically, most people, when considering growing a tree, start off by thinking about the space in which they want to grow it. So, we've ordered our list accordingly. At the beginning are the trees (such as guelder rose) for the small garden or space, and at the end are those (such as European lime) that require park-sized room for growth.

In other words, wherever you are in the pages ahead, you'll know that trees on adjacent pages will also be suitable for your space. It's as simple as that.

Going non-native

Having described the trees, we've also provided many suggestions for alternative species or varieties, often ornamental, that occur within the same family and which require similar growing conditions.

With the uncertainty of climate change and the fact that more of us than ever live in towns and cities, we want to encourage people to sow not only native trees, but also grow ornamental species that can be easily grown from seed. Because ornamental non-native trees may survive better as our climate changes – and in urban environments they have often been selected for their tolerance to pollution – they may now be the best choice for many situations. We have therefore included a selection of ornamental non-native trees, as well as native species.

4m (10 years/mature)

3m (5 years)

Guelder Rose

Viburnum opulus

This native, deciduous, multi-stemmed shrub or small tree can grow to a height of 4m. It is found naturally in woodland, scrub and hedgerows, especially on lime-rich soils.

The main stems of this plant carry the flower buds, which develop into flower heads in June and July. The flower heads have large, sterile outer flowers, and smaller, yellow inner ones, which are fertile. Once pollinated, the plant develops bright red berries in the autumn, each containing a single seed. The berries are eaten by birds, which distribute the seeds in their droppings at a distance from the parent plant.

The combination of colourful berries and leaves that turn a vivid red in October have made the guelder rose a popular ornamental shrub for gardens. This has led to the development of a range of ornamental varieties.

Growing well in moist soils, the guelder rose occurs on soils from both moderately acid to alkaline, but is most commonly found on the latter. Needing light to flower, this is not a shade-loving species.

Seed guide

Collect the ripe, red fruits. Remove the seeds from the fruit and wash thoroughly. Stratify the seeds for one winter, or two. Select and sow germinating seeds in the first or second spring.

Did you know?

The name 'guelder', comes from the Netherlands, where a particularly fine variety of this plant arose.

The alternate shiny, untoothed leaves have seven to nine veins. The berries turn from green to red, then purple-black

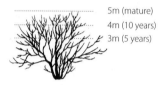

5m (mature)
4m (10 years)
3m (5 years)

Alder Buckthorn

Frangula alnus

The native alder buckthorn is a shrub or small tree, which grows on peaty soils in damp woods and bogs. It is not related to either alder or buckthorn, but can be found growing with alder in wet woodlands. It has attractive autumn colours.

This species had a wide range of uses. The wood was used to prepare charcoal, due to its slow-burning nature. Its berries, which ripen from green to red to black, were used for dyes and also as a purgative, along with its bark.

Its berries, which ripen from green to red to black, were used for wool dyes – the unripe berries producing green and yellow shades, whilst the ripe berries produce blue-grey, blue and green shades.

The plant also has purgative qualities like buckthorn, but was more often used on animals.

Seed guide

Collect the fruits before they are fully ripe, from late summer to early autumn. Remove the seeds from the fruit and wash thoroughly. Stratify the seeds, usually for one winter, occasionally two. Select and sow germinating seeds in spring.

Did you know?

Charcoal from this tree was an important part of gunpowder-making.

Opposite leaves, with small irregular 'teeth' around the margin. The fruit is a pink capsule containing four orange seeds

6m (mature)

4m (10 years)

2m (5 years)

European Spindle

Euonymus europaeus

A native deciduous shrub or small tree, the European spindle can grow to a height of 6m. Fairly inconspicuous most of the year, spindle comes into its own in the autumn, with its opposite leaves turning a glorious red colour, offset by its striking pinky-red seed capsules, which contain bright orange seeds. Unfortunately, these berries are poisonous and can cause problems if they are eaten.

Growing in hedges and wood edges, and thriving on chalky or salt-poor soils, plus good deep rich soils, spindle has become a popular plant in parks and gardens.

Historically dyes were made of the berries. Three colours were obtained – green by boiling the seeds with alum; yellow by boiling the seeds alone and red from the seed capsules. Skewers were also made from the branches for butchers and cooks, and the leaves, dried and powdered, were said to drive vermin away from children's heads.

Seed guide

Collect the seeds from the pods and stratify them for 16 weeks outdoors. Sow the seeds in the spring in a seedbed.

Did you know?

The wood of the spindle is very hard and, in the past, was used for making spindles for spinning wool.

The large opposite leaves have dense white hairs underneath. The berries turn from red to blue-black as they ripen

6m (mature)

4m (10 years)
3m (5 years)

Wayfaring Tree

Viburnum lantana

This small, deciduous, multi-stemmed shrub or small tree occurs naturally in Britain, and can reach a height of 6m. It occurs in hedgerows and scrubby areas, as well as woodland edges.

The flower heads occur at the ends of the stems, and consist of clusters of small white flowers. Once pollinated by bees and other insects, the fruits begin to ripen from July to September. The clusters of berries turn from green, through red to black as they ripen. The berries each contain a single seed, which are dispersed when they are eaten by birds.

The wayfaring tree grows well on lime-rich soils, but not where the soil is waterlogged.

Seed guide

Collect the ripe, blueish-black fruit. Remove the seeds from the fruit and wash them thoroughly. Stratify the seeds for one winter, or two. Select and sow germinating seeds in the first or second spring.

Did you know?

The wayfaring tree was named by the 16th-century botanist John Gerard from the Latin '*vibernum*', from which its French name '*viorne lantane*' was derived.

Small dull green leaves grow on dark thorny twigs. The blue-black sloes are very distinctive

7m (mature)
6m (10 years)

3m (5 years)

Blackthorn

Prunus spinosa

This widespread shrubby species can often be found on woodland edges and occurs on a wide range of soils. It occasionally grows into a small tree and its spiny twigs make it a good hedging plant.

The wood can be turned into walking sticks or, in Ireland, into a cudgel known as a shillelagh. The blue-black berries, known as sloes, are used to flavour gin or can be made into jam.

In the 18th and early 19th century blackthorn leaves were used as a substitute for Chinese tea, which was expensive at the time. Blackthorn leaves were considered to be the best European alternative to tea, as the plant contains a chemical that when boiled was said to resemble the 'delicate perfume of green tea'.

Flying insects are attracted to the early flowers produced by the species. The caterpillar of the black hairstreak butterfly feeds on the leaves.

Seed guide

Collect the fruit (sloes) from the bush after the leaves have fallen, from September onwards. Remove the seeds from the flesh and wash thoroughly. Stratify the seeds, usually for one winter. In cool autumns, germination can be improved by keeping stratifying seeds at room temperature for two weeks, before putting them outside for the winter. Select and sow germinating seeds in spring.

Did you know?

Shillelaghs – traditionally made from blackthorn – were Irish weapons, used to settle arguments or disputes.

Small shiny evergreen leaves, which grow in opposite pairs. The fruit is a small capsule containing black seeds

9m (mature)

6m (10 years)

2m (5 years)

Box

Buxus sempervirens

This slow-growing shrub or small evergreen tree can reach a maximum height of about 9m. It is a native of western Europe and is probably a native of England although, as it was used extensively in Britain by the Romans in their gardens, it may have spread naturally from Roman settlements.

Box can be found growing wild in southern England, the most famous sites being Box Hill in Surrey, where it grows with yew and large-leaved lime, and in the Chilterns.

The evergreen leaves persist for five or six years, and box has frequently been used as hedging material or for topiary.

Box wood is very dense and fine grained and is so heavy that it sinks in water when it is green. Because the wood is very close to ivory in texture, it was used extensively for turning and inlay.

Seed guide

The tree's fruits are three-celled capsules, with each cell containing two seeds. They split along six lines, expelling the shiny, black, smooth seeds. Collect the seed capsules when they are ripe and keep them in a paper bag until they open. Sow in a pot or seedbed immediately (although stratification through the winter can improve germination rates).

Did you know?

Unfortunately, freshly cut box smells like a tom cat's urine.

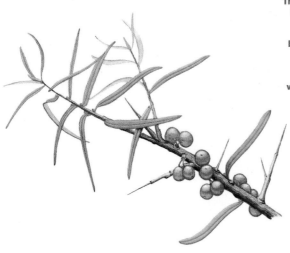

The thin willow-like leaves are covered with silver hairs below, and are dark green on top. The berries are a vibrant orange

9m (mature)

6m (10 years)

3m (5 years)

Sea Buckthorn

Hippophae rhamnoides

A native shrub growing to a height of 9m, sea buckthorn occurs naturally along the east coast and has been planted in other coastal locations.

It is a very hardy species, which is both salt and drought resistant. Because it suckers well, it spreads easily and has been used to stabilise extensive sand-dune areas.

The dense branches are spiny, with silvery-green leaves. The berries, which are bright orange and rich in vitamin C, are attractive to birds, and are an important foodstuff for migrating thrushes arriving along the east coast in the autumn.

The oil derived from the berries has had a wide range of medicinal uses. This is because the berries also contain vitamin E and beta-carotene. These components, along with vitamin C, are anti-oxidants, forming a vital part of the body's defence system.

Seed guide

Collect the ripe berries from September to December, and separate the seeds from the flesh. Wash the seeds thoroughly and stratify them for at least 12 weeks. In spring, collect the germinating seeds and plant out in pots or a seedbed.

Did you know?

The beautiful orange colour from the berries can be extracted using hot water, and has been used as a dye for wool.

The leaves consist of three-lobed leaflets, rather like a clover leaf. The fruit has brown 'pea-like' pods containing black poisonous seeds

9m (mature)

6m (10 years)

2m (5 years)

Laburnum

Laburnum anagyroides

A small deciduous tree or large shrub, laburnum seldom exceeds 9m in height. This tree is in the same botanical order as the pea family, which explains its yellow hanging 'pea' flowers and three-leaflet leaves. Laburnum grows well on most soils, provided they are not overdry. It requires a sunny position, and does well in sandy soils.

Introduced to Britain in 1596 by the famous gardener and plant collector Tradescant, it can now be found growing widely throughout the country.

Unfortunately, for such a widely grown tree, its seeds are poisonous and contain a highly toxic alkaloid – cytisine. Cytisine's side effects can include nausea and, in larger doses, even death via respiratory failure. One report showed that 10 seeds were fatal to a child.

The heartwood of laburnum gets darker when exposed to light, becoming chocolate brown. This rich colour, combined with its wide use by cabinetmakers, made it in 1812 'the most valuable timber grown in Scotland'.

Seed guide

The brown seed pods are about 5cm long, and split to reveal small black poisonous seeds. Collect the ripe pods in September/October before they split open. In March, puncture the hard, water-impermeable seed coat with a file or knife – without damaging the embryo within; alternatively cover the seeds in about five times their volume of boiling water and allow to cool for 12 hours. Sow chipped or swollen seeds in an outdoor seedbed in March or April.

Did you know?

Oddly for a poisonous plant, laburnum was widely used for hedging in Ceredigion, as well as Carmarthenshire, in Wales. (See, for example, the A487 between Llanarth and Cardigan.)

An evergreen tree with alternate leaves and toothed edges. The main vein of the leaf is white. The reddish fruit is like a rough strawberry

10m (mature)

7m (10 years)

2m (5 years)

Strawberry Tree

Arbutus unedo

This is a small tree, which tends to grow to 10m in height and 3m in girth, generally reaching its largest size in Ireland. It is found growing wild in parts of the West of Ireland, but is generally thought of as a shrub in the Mediterranean.

It is difficult to be certain when the species was introduced to mainland Britain, but some evidence suggests that it arrived in the middle of the 16th century.

This tree's flowers appear in autumn, in short drooping groups. The fruit ripens in the autumn following flowering, resulting in there being the current year's flowers and last year's berries simultaneously. The stalked berry resembles a strawberry, hence the name, but is, in fact, very different.

In order to thrive, this tree needs warm conditions in winter and damp conditions in summer. Although *Arbutus* is easily raised from seed, the seedlings suffer from cold winds and frost damage. Young plants therefore benefit from being kept under glass.

Seed guide

Collect the ripe, red fruits. Carefully remove the tiny seeds from the flesh and wash thoroughly. Stratify the seeds, usually for one winter, and sow them in a pot or seedbed in the spring.

Did you know?

The tree's Latin name is '*unedo*', from the meaning 'I eat one'. This is because, although the berries look like strawberries, you can only eat one as they taste fairly disgusting.

The blue-green needles are spiky and have a distinctive white band on their upper surface. The blue-grey berries are in fact fleshy cones

10m (mature)

5m (10 years)

2m (5 years)

Common Juniper

Juniperus communis

A small evergreen coniferous tree or large shrub, common juniper grows to a height of 10m. One of the most widely distributed trees in northern Europe, its distribution in Britain is curious, being found on the chalk and limestone of southern England and in the uplands of Wales, northern England and Scotland.

With a wide range of medicinal and culinary uses, juniper is perhaps best known for its 'berries', which are used to flavour gin. Oddly, the berries are, in fact, small cones – with a coating which ripens to a blue-black colour – containing six fused scales, each scale being a single seed. Like other real berries, the purpose of the outer coating is to induce birds to eat the fruit and then drop the seeds some distance from the parent tree.

Naturally occurring in a wide range of forms, juniper has been widely cultivated for gardens, particularly in its many dwarf and prostrate types.

This tree can grow on a wide range of well-drained soils.

Seed guide

Collect the seeds from the bush, remove them from the flesh and wash thoroughly. Stratify the seeds, although they may take two winters to germinate. Collecting green seeds can speed up the process, allowing them to germinate after one winter. Once germinated, sow in a pot or a seedbed.

Did you know?

The juniper carpet is a scarce moth species, which feeds on junipers. It naturally occurs in only a few localities throughout Britain, although it can occasionally be discovered feeding on junipers in residential gardens.

And in a similar vein...

There are other junipers for you to try

Variegated Chinese juniper

Prostrate Rocky Mountain juniper

(R) Alligator juniper

The leaves have pointed tips with smooth undersides and toothed edges. The small green apples ripen during September

10m (mature)

7m (10 years)

3m (5 years)

Crab Apple

Malus sylvestris

The crab apple is a tree of hedges, copses and oak woodlands, thriving in fertile and heavy soils. It often grows singly, with large distances between individual trees.

The crab apple was the original ancestor of some domesticated apple varieties, which were produced from it by careful selection. Historically, when a new variety was being developed, the wild crab apple rootstock was used.

The wood of this species was used for engraving and for making set squares and other drawing instruments. Crab apples can also be used for jams, wine and a fermented apple juice called verjuice.

The tree has high wildlife value, attracting insects to its spring flowers. Its small, bitter fruits provide birds and mammals with food in the autumn. The tree also provides excellent growing conditions for mistletoe.

Seed guide

Collect the fruit from the tree or the ground when it turns yellow-orange. If you can hear the 'pips' rattle when you shake the apple, it is ripe. Cut open the apple, and if the seeds are brown this confirms its ripeness. Carefully remove the seeds and stratify them, usually for one winter. In cool autumns, germination can be improved by keeping stratifying seeds at room temperature for two weeks, before putting them outside for the winter. Select and sow germinating seeds in spring.

Did you know?

The rootstocks of commercially grown 'eating' apples are often derived from the crab apple.

And in a similar vein…

There are several other crab apples for you to try

'Golden Hornet' crab apple

'Dartmouth' crab apple

(R) 'Echtermeyer' crab apple

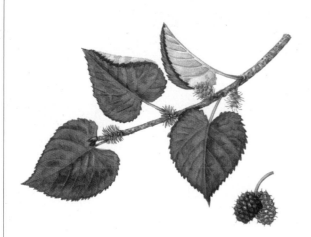

The large heart-shaped leaves are hairy on both sides. The fruit is a deep, wine-red colour when ripe

10m (mature)
8m (10 years)

3m (5 years)

Black Mulberry

Morus nigra

The black mulberry has been widely planted in southern England for its fruit, but becomes rarer as one travels north. It originated in Asia and was first introduced to Britain in the 14th century. In 1609, King James I increased the number planted in Britain in order to build up the silk industry, in the mistaken belief that silkworms fed on the leaves of the tree. In fact, silkworms favour the white mulberry (*Morus alba*), which does not appear to like the British climate greatly and remains uncommon.

The black mulberry grows well in parks and gardens and can be raised from seed. However, the more commonly-used way of growing new trees is to take a 'truncheon' – a 2m length of branch – which is driven 1m into the ground. It will then sprout to produce a new tree.

The wood is hard, and valued for furniture and veneers. However, it is a scarce wood and little used. The large, black raspberry-like fruits are tasty to humans and birds alike.

Seed guide

Black mulberries are a similar shape and colour to raspberries. They fall from the tree when they are ripe and should be collected quickly before they are eaten by birds and animals. Squeeze the incredibly sticky fruits in your hands to release the seeds and wash them thoroughly. Stratify the seeds, usually for one winter, and inspect regularly. Select and sow germinating seeds from late winter onwards.

Did you know?

The nursery rhyme 'Here We Go Round the Mulberry Bush' is thought to have arisen at Wakefield Prison, where prisoners exercised around a large mulberry standing in the grounds.

The light green leaves have fine regular teeth. The black cherries contain a single hard stone

10m (mature)

7m (10 years)

3m (5 years)

Bird Cherry

Prunus padus

Bird cherry is found in the north and west, growing wild in Scotland, Ireland, Wales, northern England and parts of the Midlands. It is most widespread by limestone streams in the Scottish glens, the Lake District and in the Pennines. It is grown in the south of England in streets and gardens for its attractive white flowers.

The reddish-brown heartwood was used in cabinet making and woodturning, while extracts from the bark were used for medicinal purposes. The bitter black cherries were also used to flavour brandies and wines.

Its outstanding May flowers provide food for many insect species and its cherries are eaten by a variety of birds and small mammals in the summer.

Seed guide

Collect the fruits from the tree by hand, when the fruit turns black. Carefully remove the seeds from the flesh and wash thoroughly. Stratify the seeds, usually for one winter. With later collections, germination can be improved by keeping stratifying seeds at room temperature for two weeks, before putting them outside for the winter. Select and sow germinating seeds in spring.

Did you know?

One place where bird cherry grows is Wayland Wood in Norfolk. This wood is famous as the origin of the 'Babes in the Wood' legend, where two children were abandoned by their fortune-hunting uncle.

The Teacher's Tale

Paul Cook has been a Tree Warden for two years, ever since he first found out about the role at a Pembrokeshire seed-gathering event. Yet Paul has gone a step further in his involvement with trees: they're now the basis of his business, and what a wonderful business it is.

'I'd worked for many years at a day centre for people with learning disabilities,' he says, 'and realised that many of the users of the centre were missing out on one of the great aspects of life while they were there. They weren't getting to see the great outdoors.'

Paul took his centre users on day trips out to National Trust properties, helping out with volunteering work, and saw immediately the benefit it had for them. Before long, he'd set up Esteam. It's a workers' cooperative, with its own tree nursery. 'The team collects the seeds, plants them, then we sell the saplings on to nurseries,' he explains. 'We've also got a workshop for recycled wood, and we recycle tools to send on to countries such as Tanzania that desperately need them.'

Esteam has only been going for a couple of years, but Paul already has a team of over 30 people who work there. Most have learning disabilities, some are on probation, but all get a real kick out of their work.

'For many of the team, it's a wonderful way of seeing first-hand how something works,' says Paul. 'They pick up seeds, bring them back, stratify them, plant them, then see them growing. It gives them a great sense of ownership, and it's wonderful to see them become calmer about life in general. They have a place, and a role, which helps them feel that they really belong.

'It's wonderful that trees can help people in such an enriching way.'

Over to you

If you too would like to become a volunteer Tree Warden, turn to page 246 for more information.

The leaves have finely-toothed edges, and veins which point to the tip. The black berries are found in clusters

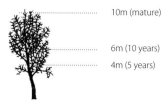

10m (mature)

6m (10 years)

4m (5 years)

Buckthorn

Rhamnus catharticus

The buckthorn is a shrub of the chalk and limestone of southern and central England. It grows in hedgerows or as scrub on downland and can occasionally form into small trees.

Buckthorn is one of the favoured food plants of the brimstone butterfly and the berries are eaten by birds.

Historically the inner bark was used to induce vomiting, and the berries have a purgative effect, leading to one of the plant's common names – purging buckthorn. So strong is that purgative quality that it was said that even the flesh of the birds that had eaten the berries could bring on the desired effects.

Dyes were also once made from this plant – the ripe berries being used to produce a green dye and the bark a beautiful yellow colour.

Seed guide

To beat the birds, collect the fruits before they are fully ripe (ie completely black). Remove the seeds from the fruit and wash thoroughly. Stratify the seeds, usually for one winter, occasionally two. Select and sow germinating seeds in spring.

Did you know?

The name 'purging buckthorn' was given to mark the way the bark and berries were used to create a laxative although, due to their violent effect, they are now rarely used, except by vets.

The leaves consist of five to seven toothed leaflets, which smell unpleasant. The black berries develop in clusters

10m (mature)

6m (10 years)

4m (5 years)

Elder

Sambucus nigra

Elder is a large native shrub or small tree which likes soils that are nitrogen-rich, growing particularly well near abandoned buildings, churchyards and other places where organic matter has enriched the soil.

If allowed to grow into a mature tree, elder has hard wood. This was often used for pegs and toys or, occasionally, for cogs in mills when hornbeam was not available.

The flowers and berries have a wide range of culinary uses, being made into wines or jams. The flower buds can be pickled or fried in batter, or infused as a tea. Various dyes can be made from parts of the tree, while the leaves can be made into an insecticide.

The berries and flowers provide excellent food for birds and insects.

Seed guide

Collect the clusters of berries from the tree when they turn dark purple to black in August to October. Carefully squeeze the fruits to release the seeds. Then remove the seeds from the flesh and wash thoroughly. Stratify the seeds, occasionally for one winter, but often two. Select and sow germinating seeds in spring.

Did you know?

A widely used plant, elder's most famous products are the cordial or 'champagne' made from its flowers, and the wine made from its berries.

Leaves have
shallower lobes
than hawthorn,
and the red
haws contain
two seeds

12m (mature)

8m (10 years)

3m (5 years)

Midland Hawthorn

Crataegus laevigata

Midland hawthorn is the rarer of the two native hawthorn species, being found on heavy soils in shady woodlands, usually in the south east of Britain. This species grows into a small tree more regularly than hawthorn. It can be found growing along roadsides and in gardens, and many ornamental forms have been created, including 'Paul's Scarlet', which is frequently seen in towns and cities.

As with hawthorn, the wood has been used for tool handles and walking sticks, while the berries are an excellent source of vitamin C.

The stems of Midland hawthorn are often contorted, improving the walking sticks one can make from the tree, while the flowers provide nectar for spring insects. The berries provide excellent food for birds, especially thrushes, and small mammals.

Seed guide

Collect the red berries once they are ripe, from autumn onwards. Remove the seeds from the flesh and wash them thoroughly. (Soak the berries for a day or two, if the flesh is hard to remove.) Stratify the seeds, occasionally for one, but usually two winters. Select and sow germinating seeds each spring.

Did you know?

The easy way to distinguish this species from English hawthorn, is that this tree has two seeds in the berries, while the other tree has one.

The small leaves have three main lobes and two smaller basal lobes. Each pair of seeds lies almost in a straight line, and may have pink tinges

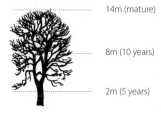

14m (mature)

8m (10 years)

2m (5 years)

Field Maple

Acer campestre

Britain's only native maple, the field maple is a species which prefers lime-rich soil, but will tolerate other conditions. It occurs naturally in hedges and as the understorey in woods and copses throughout England and Wales. It is often grown in parks and gardens because of its beautiful autumn colour and its ability to tolerate air pollution. In the past, it was used for topiary.

The wood of the field maple is soft but produces beautiful veneer, used for woodturning and furniture. Historically, it was also used to make harps.

It is an important habitat for up to 51 invertebrate species. The fruit 'keys' are often eaten by small mammals.

Seed guide

Collect the fruits from the tree in autumn, when they are brown. Stratify the seeds, usually for one winter. Select and sow germinating seeds in spring.

Did you know?

The maple prominent moth is one of the 51 species of insect which feed upon this tree.

And in a similar vein...

There are other maples for you to try

Smooth Japanese maple

Downy Japanese maple

(R) Moosewood

The large heart-shaped leaves have wavy edges. The 10cm-long brown seed pods contain flat elliptical seeds

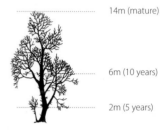

14m (mature)

6m (10 years)

2m (5 years)

Judas Tree

Cercis siliquastrum

This beautiful small deciduous tree can reach a height of 14m. It is a native of south-eastern Europe and western Asia. It was introduced to Britain in 1596 by the herbalist John Gerard.

The tree produces large numbers of bright pink pea-like flowers during the early summer, some even arising straight out of the bark of the trunk. They are pollinated by bees and, being a member of the pea family, the seed pods are pea-shaped and hang vertically.

Preferring well-drained soils, this tree dislikes wet soils. It is a tree for sunny places, disliking shade. The autumn colour can be attractive, with the leaves turning a yellow-brown colour. Unfortunately, this tree can be prone to a number of diseases, particularly coral spot and cankers.

Seed guide

Collect the ripe seed pods from the tree from September onwards. Separate the pods from the seeds, and sow immediately into pots or a seedbed. Alternatively, store the seeds in a paper bag and sow in the early spring.

Did you know?

Legend has it that this was the tree upon which Judas Iscariot hanged himself after betraying Christ – hence the name. The Latin name for the tree is derived from the word '*siliqua*', which means 'pod'.

The large
opposite leaves
are oval with a
pointed end. The
fruit is a large
cigar-shaped
seed pod which
contains brown
bean-like seeds

15m (mature)

8m (10 years)

2m (5 years)

Indian Bean Tree

Catalpa bignonioides

This medium-sized deciduous tree can grow to 15–20m and is a native of the eastern part of the United States, in Georgia and Florida. It was introduced into Britain in 1726 by Mark Catesby, who first described the tree in *Natural History of Carolina, Florida and the Bahama Islands*, stating: 'The tree was unknown to the inhabited parts of Carolina until I brought the seed from the remoter parts of the country. And though the inhabitants are little curious about gardening, yet the uncommon beauty of the tree has induced them to propagate it, and 'tis become an ornament to many in their gardens and probably will be the same to ours in England.'

The large heart-shaped leaves are late to emerge, often not occurring until May. Oddly for leaves, they secrete nectar and give off a disagreeable smell when crushed.

The tree's beautiful flowers are white and trumpet-shaped, with yellow spots inside, growing in clusters of 20-40. The seeds, for which the tree is named, occur in long thin bean-like pods and are flat and light brown, with papery wings.

Seed guide

In Britain, unfortunately, the fruit rarely ripens, so generally the tree is propagated by both softwood and root cuttings. In late spring to early summer, before the leaves are fully developed, take 10cm-long softwood cuttings, and put in a frame to grow.

Did you know?

The tree's Latin name, '*Catalpa*', is a corruption of 'Catawba', the name of a Native American tribe that formerly occupied Georgia and the Carolinas.

The leaves are soft and hairy and have saw-toothed edges with a drawn-out tip. The nuts grow in clusters of up to four each, enclosed by a leafy structure known as a bract

15m (mature)

12m (10 years)

7m (5 years)

Hazel

Corylus avellana

This medium-sized deciduous tree, reaching a height of 15m, is found throughout Britain, growing in woods and hedgerows on a wide range of soils, including chalk, limestone, mildly acid soils and clays. The male catkins often appear in January or February, adding the first splash of colour to the winter woodlands.

Hazel is usually coppiced to produce thin flexible poles, which are used for fencing, hurdles, pea and bean sticks, and thatching spars.

Coppiced hazel woodlands are rich in wildlife, as the regular cutting allows light to reach the woodland floor, which benefits flowers and butterflies. More than 106 invertebrate species have been found on this tree. Mammals feed on the hazelnuts, which are particularly attractive to squirrels and dormice.

Seed guide

Collect the first fruits in autumn as they ripen from green to brown, but be careful that the squirrels don't beat you to it. Sow immediately in a pot or seedbed; protect from predators and severe frost.

Did you know?

Hazel is the main element of wattle and daub construction, which has been used in Britain for at least 6,000 years. Wattle and daub consists of hazel woven between 'wattle' uprights to create a latticework, and covered or 'daubed' with a mixture of clay/sand – and sometimes cow dung – to exclude the wind.

And in a similar vein...

There are several other hazels for you to try

'Contorted' hazel

'Heterophylla' hazel

(R) 'Golden' hazel

The leaves have deeply-divided lobes. The fleshy red haws contain a single seed

15m (mature)

12m (10 years)

3m (5 years)

Hawthorn

Crataegus monogyna

The native hawthorn grows throughout the UK, apart from the extreme north-west of Scotland. It tolerates a very wide range of soils, except peat, and is probably best known as a plant of hedgerows.

The wood has been used for tool handles and walking sticks, while the berries are an excellent source of vitamin C.

Hawthorn has a high wildlife value, as its flowers provide nectar for spring insects, while its berries provide excellent food for birds, especially thrushes, and small mammals.

Usually thought of as a hedging plant, hawthorn can grow to become a lovely medium-sized tree if uncut.

The May blossom of the hawthorn has become associated with many rituals and stories. They were regarded as symbols of hope and their scent was thought to be not only reviving to the spirit, but would drive off poisons. It was even thought that wearing a sprig of hawthorn in your hat could protect you from lightning.

Seed guide

Collect the red berries once they are ripe, from autumn onwards. Remove the seeds from the flesh and wash them thoroughly. (Soak the berries for a day or two, if the flesh is hard to remove.) Stratify the seeds, occasionally for one, but usually two winters. Select and sow germinating seeds each spring.

Did you know?

The oldest hawthorn tree in Britain is thought to be the Hethel thorn in Norfolk, which is considered to be more than 700 years old. This tree is also Britain's smallest nature reserve at 0.025ha.

And in a similar vein...

There are several other hawthorns for you to try

Quebec hawthorn

Crataegus pseudoheterophylla

(R) Azarole hawthorn

15m (mature)

8m (10 years)

2m (5 years)

Holly

Ilex aquifolium

The holly is a very widespread native tree, which grows on almost any soil. It tolerates shade well and often grows as the understorey in woodlands, but also likes open situations and occurs widely in hedgerows.

Its hard, white wood takes stain well and was traditionally known as 'English ebony'. It was particularly used for carving and inlay, while the shoots with berries are used for Christmas decorations.

There are male and female holly trees, which leads to one of the most commonly asked questions – 'Why doesn't my holly produce berries?' This will either be because the tree is male, or because there are no male trees in the area to produce pollen to fertilise the female.

The berries are eaten by birds and the foliage by deer and rabbits. Holly is also the food plant of the holly blue butterfly, but only nine other invertebrate species have been found feeding on this tree.

Seed guide

Collect the ripe, red berries from the tree in winter. Remove the seeds from the flesh and wash them thoroughly. Soak the berries for a day or two, if the flesh is hard to remove. Stratify the seed for one or more winters. Select and sow germinating seeds each spring.

Did you know?

The Hampshire town of Ringwood was built upon the site of a very large circular holly wood. Such circular woods are known in the New Forest as 'ringwoods'.

And in a similar vein...

There are other hollies for you to try

Holly 'Aurifodina'

Perry's weeping holly

(R) Holly 'Watereriana'

The dark glossy leaves have smaller teeth than crab apples, with a longer leaf stalk. The small green pears ripen and contain brown seeds

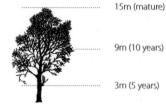

15m (mature)

9m (10 years)

3m (5 years)

Wild Pear

Pyrus communis

The wild pear can be found scattered alongside road verges, in hedgerows and on woodland edges throughout Britain. It is also planted in parks and gardens. It is an uncommon tree, and may actually be rare, as many supposed wild pears are actually 'wildings' – trees descended from domesticated pears. The wild tree has spiny branches and produces small gritty pears. The dark brown bark also cracks into distinctive plates.

The pale pink wood takes stain easily and was used for veneers, woodturning, carving and for making musical instruments, including flutes and – when stained – black piano keys.

The flowers of the wild pear attract insects in the spring, although to the human nose they smell fishy. The tree also provides excellent growing conditions for mistletoe.

Seed guide

Collect the fruit from the tree or the ground when ripe. Cut open the pear, and if the seeds are brown this confirms that they are ripe. Carefully remove the seeds and stratify them, usually for one winter. In cool autumns, germination can be improved by keeping stratifying seeds at room temperature for two weeks, before putting them outside for the winter. Select and sow germinating seeds in spring.

Did you know?

Another pear species grows in Plymouth. Called the Plymouth pear (*Pyrus cordata*), it is protected under Schedule 8 of the Wildlife and Countryside Act 1981 and is the only tree protected because of its rarity. It is also listed in the British Red Data Book of Endangered Species.

The Tree-hunter's Tale

'Daddy, did you always want to be a tree-hunter?' When Tree Warden Rob McBride's young daughter asks him this question, as she often does, he smiles. 'The answer to that question is no,' he explains, 'but now that I am, it's changed my life.'

Rob's background isn't in trees, but IT, the profession he was pursuing until he fell victim to illness in 2004. As he emerged from his enforced absence from work, someone mentioned to him the possibility of Tree Wardening, and a Woodland Trust campaign called the Ancient Tree Hunt. 'Initially, I took on the role as a form of therapy, but as time has passed, I've become hooked. You discover things on your doorstep that no one's really noticed before.'

The Ancient Tree Hunt is a nationwide search for trees that are part of our heritage. The idea is to build a database of ancient, veteran and notable trees up and down the country, campaign for their protection, and raise awareness of the historical importance, and sheer magnificence, of these living history books. This reinforces The Tree Council's Green Monuments Campaign.

Rob is a verifier, which means that when someone posts a record of a tree on the website (www.ancienttreehunt.org.uk) in the Ellesmere area of Shropshire where he lives, it's Rob who goes out to check the details. 'The sense of excitement about discovering something new is always high,' he says. 'That goes for people, as well as trees. I remember once going out tree-hunting with a trainee druid, a psychic and two farmers. We found some wonderful old trees, and swapped some great stories.'

Rob's life has come full circle. He's now using his IT skills to record these trees onto the database and he also posts his tree hunting videos onto youtube.com (search for 'treehunter'). 'Did I always want to be a tree-hunter?' he smiles. 'I do now.'

Over to you

If you too would like to become a volunteer Tree Warden, turn to page 246 for more information.

The alternate leaves have a covering of thick white hairs underneath. The berries, which are at first green, ripen to bright red

15m (mature)

8m (10 years)

3m (5 years)

Whitebeam

Sorbus aria

The whitebeam is a native tree which prefers chalk and lime-rich soils, but it also tolerates other soil types. Its ability to withstand pollution means it has become a widely-planted urban tree. However, such trees are often ornamental forms of the wild species and are unlikely to produce reasonable seed.

The tree's hard, tough wood was used to make machinery cogs. Its overripe berries can be turned into jelly to accompany venison.

As with all *Sorbus* trees, the berries are eaten by birds. The flowers attract insects, and the white caterpillar of a tiny *Argynesthia* moth feeds on the shoots and flower buds.

Seed guide

Collect bunches of fruits when they turn crimson. Remove the seeds from the flesh and wash thoroughly. Stratify the seeds, usually for one winter. In cool autumns, germination can be improved by keeping stratifying seeds at room temperature for two weeks, before putting them outside for the winter. Select and sow germinating seeds in spring.

Did you know?

The tree was often planted as a boundary marker, as the white underside of its leaves flashing in the wind drew attention to it.

Each leaf consists of numerous pairs of stalkless leaflets. It has distinctive red berries

15m (mature)

8m (10 years)

3m (5 years)

Rowan

Sorbus aucuparia

Rowan is found throughout Britain, growing naturally at altitudes of up to 1,000m in Scotland. It is a tree of mountains, woodlands and valleys, growing on a wide range of soils, including chalks, acid soils and even peat. It has been widely planted in parks, gardens and streets due to its striking red berries, which occur as early as July, and its autumn foliage.

Its timber is strong, hard and flexible, leading to its use in tools and carving, and for shortbows, which were favoured mainly by the Welsh. The berries were turned into a jelly, said to be excellent with cold game or wildfowl, and a wholesome 'perry' or cider can also be made from them.

The tree has excellent wildlife values, providing fruit for thrushes and blackbirds, which aid the rowan in colonising new areas by eating the seeds and dispersing them around the countryside.

Seed guide

To beat the birds, collect the ripening clusters of berries from late August. Carefully remove the seeds from the flesh and wash thoroughly. Stratify the seeds, usually for one winter. In cool autumns, germination can be improved by keeping stratifying seeds at room temperature for two weeks, before putting them outside for the winter. Select and sow germinating seeds in spring.

Did you know?

This tree was often planted to keep witches away from houses and churches.

And in a similar vein...

There are several other whitebeams for you to try

Lesser whitebeam

Devon whitebeam

(R) Swedish whitebeam

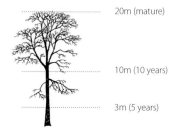

20m (mature)

10m (10 years)

3m (5 years)

Handkerchief Tree

Davidia involucrata

This medium-sized deciduous tree, which can reach a height of 20m, is a native of China. It arrived in Britain in 1902, brought by the plant hunter Ernest Wilson after a dangerous journey in which his boat sank in rapids and his guide was an opium addict.

The tree had first been reported by Father David (see right) in 1869. He wrote about its spectacular white flowers, which have made it desirable in parks and gardens. The flowers are composed of two large white bracts surrounding a purple cluster of flowers. These flowers have given the tree its English name, and also its alternate name of the dove tree, as the bracts blow in the wind like a bird's wing.

The fruit is a hard green nut containing three to five seeds.

Growing well on moist, well-drained soil, it is a tree that likes full sun or partial shade, protected from strong winds.

Seed guide

Collect the nuts from the tree in October, when they turn reddish brown. Each nut will contain three to five seeds. Wash the fruit and mix with damp compost in June/July. Store the mixture in a large pot and keep the compost moist. After 12-20 weeks, the nuts will have split and the young roots will have emerged. Plant these young seedlings out in the autumn.

Did you know?

Davidia is named after French missionary and naturalist Father David, who lived in China in the 19th century. He was the first westerner to describe the giant panda (*Ailuropoda melanoleuca*).

Leaves are alternate and are composed of 14-28 leaflets. The brown pods contain bean-like seeds

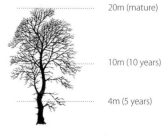

20m (mature)

10m (10 years)

4m (5 years)

Honey Locust

Gleditsia triacanthos

This deciduous tree can grow to 20m and is native to the north and east of the United States. It arrived in Britain during the later half of the 17th century, at Fulham, London.

The stem and branches have sharp spines and the seed pods are long and bean-shaped. The leaves are made up of 14-28 leaflets, and the bark has deep cracks and fissures. Turning a deep gold colour in autumn, it is a good ornamental tree for parks and large gardens. The wood is hard and strong, and has been used for fence posts and rails in the US.

Although called honey locust, the tree does not produce a great deal of honey. However, the seed pods are very sweet and are much prized by cattle, who like eating them, usually when they have fallen to the ground.

This tree tolerates pollution, heat, drought and saline conditions. This ability, combined with its ease of transplantation, have made it a good urban tree. Its only problem is that, like the false acacia, its branches are brittle and can be broken by wind.

Seed guide

Collect the seeds in September from the tree or the ground, when the pods are red/brown and ripe. Put the pods in a paper bag at room temperature to air-dry them. This causes them to release their seeds, which should be kept in paper bags. In March puncture the hard, water-impermeable seed coat with a file or knife, without damaging the embryo within. Alternatively, cover the seeds in about five times their volume of boiling water and allow to cool for 12 hours. Sow chipped or swollen seeds in an outdoor seedbed in March or April.

Did you know?

The Native American Cherokee tribe of Tennessee made its bows from this tree.

The leaves are leathery and shiny on the upper surface. The fruits are long, oval and blue-black, with small ribbed seeds within

20m (mature)

7m (10 years)

2m (5 years)

Black Tupelo Tree

Nyssa sylvatica

A medium-sized deciduous tree which can reach a height of 20m, the black tupelo is native to the east coast of the United States. It is uncommon in Britain, although it has been grown here for at least 200 years. There are now two main varieties of this tree described: var. *sylvatica* (black tupelo) and var. *biflora* (swamp tupelo). These were historically thought of as two species – the swamp form being introduced into Britain in 1739, with the black form arriving here in 1824. They differ in their habitats: black tupelo growing on light-textured soils, and swamp tupelo on wet, heavy organic or clay soils.

This handsome, ornamental tree has a moderate growth rate and is an excellent food source for wildlife, providing good quantities of nectar for bees.

In autumn the leaves turn a brilliant scarlet, provided the tree is growing in full sun. These beautiful colours make it a very desirable tree for parks and large gardens.

It is a species which is generally found on wet soils, although it can grow in loamy soil.

Seed guide

Seed production is very variable in this species and is uncommon in Britain. If seed is produced, it ripens in September and October, and drops from September through November. The fleshy fruit surrounding the seeds is blue-black. This needs to be separated from the seeds within and the small ribbed seeds need to be washed. Stratify the collected seeds for between four and 16 weeks. The germinating seeds should be planted in pots in the spring.

Did you know?

The black fruits are high in fat and fibre and, in the US, are eaten by many birds and animals.

The needles of the tree are dark green on their upperside and a lighter green underneath. The red fleshy fruit contains a dark single seed

20m (mature)

4m (10 years)
2m (5 years)

Yew

Taxus baccata

The oldest tree in Britain is probably a yew growing in the churchyard of Fortingall, Perthshire, thought to be 5,000 years old. Many other ancient yews can be found in churchyards throughout Britain.

In the wild, yew prefers lime-rich soils and can, along with beech, become the dominant woodland type.

Its hard, colourful wood has an excellent finish and is used for a wide range of ornamental furniture, cabinets and bowls. Historically, yew produced the finest longbows, enabling archers to fire arrows over considerable distances.

The wildlife value of this species is limited, as the tree casts deep shade and few plants grow underneath it. The tree itself supports a limited number of insects. Birds also eat the red berries through the winter.

Seed guide

Collect fruit from the tree when the outer berry is a bright red colour. Remember, the seed contained within the red flesh is poisonous.

Remove the flesh and stratify the seeds for at least two winters. Select and sow germinating seeds in early spring of the second and successive years. Yew seeds take a long time to stratify, and the seedlings are also very slow growing.

Did you know?

Yew is now a rare species throughout the world, and Britain has more ancient yews than anywhere else on the planet.

And in a similar vein...

There are several other yews for you to try

Plum yew

Chinese plum yew

(R) Golden Irish yew

The rounded leaves often have a notch at their end and have seven pairs of distinctive white veins underneath. The female fruit is a green cone which turns black after the seed is shed

25m (mature)

18m (10 years)

5m (5 years)

Common Alder

Alnus glutinosa

This native alder grows in wet places, particularly on wet clays, on marshes and by lakes and fens. It is able to survive on these sites – which generally lack the nitrates needed for growth – as its roots have nodules which contain nitrogen-fixing bacteria that extract nitrogen from the air.

The timber of alder was highly valued as, unlike many woods, it does not rot quickly when exposed to continual wetting and drying. In consequence, sluice gates and canal fittings, such as locks and gates, were made from alder. Alder wood was also made into charcoal and used in the manufacture of gunpowder.

The tree has a high conservation value as the seeds provide good winter food for redpolls, siskins and other seed eaters. There are also up to 141 invertebrate species which feed on alder trees.

Seed guide

Alder cones can be collected from the lower branches of trees before they open. Place the cones in a paper bag and allow to air-dry at room temperature. As the cones open they will release the small winged seeds, which can be sown immediately. Cover with a thin layer of sharp sand and leave over winter to germinate the following spring.

Did you know?

When the wood of alder is cut it turns red-orange, which has led to superstitions that the tree bleeds – resulting in the tree's association with evil spirits.

And in a similar vein…

There are several other alders for you to try

Alnus acuminata

'Birch-leaved' alder

(R) Grey alder

The leaves are spiky and triangular and are closely arranged around the branches. The large seeds are contained within the spiky cone

25m (mature)

6m (10 years)

2m (5 years)

Monkey Puzzle

Araucaria araucana

The monkey puzzle is a tall evergreen tree, reaching a height of 25m, with a cylindrical stem, which can be 1-2m in diameter.

A native of Chile, it was introduced into Britain by Archibald Menzies. While on an expedition, which reached the coast of Chile in 1795, Menzies took seeds 'from the dessert table of the Governor' which he later planted, bringing the seedlings back to Britain.

The local Chilean population has eaten large quantities of the seeds, both roasted and boiled – their nutty flavour being reminiscent of almonds. Unfortunately, however, a large percentage of the native forests have been destroyed due to logging, fire and grazing. In consequence the tree was declared a Natural Monument in Chile, meaning that logging is now forbidden.

The tree prefers a deep well-drained soil and dislikes atmospheric pollution, but will tolerate coastal conditions.

Seed guide

Collect ripe seeds from the ground. Separate the large seeds and lay them singly in pots, with their thick end in the centre. Cover with soil. They will germinate best in a frame or cold greenhouse, where they can be protected from mice and frost.

The young plants should not remain in pots for more than a year or two as the taproot needs room to grow. However, because they can be damaged by frost, ideally the young trees should not be permanently planted out until they are at least 50cm tall.

Did you know?

The tree's name arose when the owner of a young specimen remarked: 'It would puzzle a monkey to climb that' – and the name stuck.

25m (mature)

18m (10 years)

5m (5 years)

Silver Birch

Betula pendula

The white-barked native silver birch prefers drier conditions than downy birch, and is most widespread in the south and east of Britain, on light dry soils. It grows on heathlands and woodlands and is often planted in gardens and parks. A mature birch can produce up to one million seeds.

The strong white wood was used for bobbins, flooring and schoolmasters' canes. The bark was used for paper, shoes and roofing. Current uses include parquet floors, backing for veneers, furniture and broom handles.

Birch has a high conservation value as it provides food and shelter for a wide range of birds, including redpolls and siskins. Up to 334 invertebrate species have been recorded in birches.

Seed guide

Birch cones can be collected from the lower branches of trees. Place the cones in a paper bag and allow them to dry at room temperature. Ripe cones will disintegrate on drying, leaving a mixture of tiny winged seeds, plus *fleur-de-lys*-shaped bracts. Don't bother trying to separate them! The tiny seeds can be sown immediately and should be covered with a thin layer of sharp sand, and left over winter until they germinate the following spring.

Did you know?

The rising sap of the birch in spring is sweet like that of the maple. This sweet sap can be used to make birch wine, which goes well with cheeses or cream-based puddings.

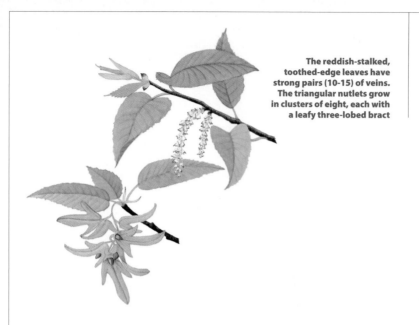

The reddish-stalked, toothed-edge leaves have strong pairs (10-15) of veins. The triangular nutlets grow in clusters of eight, each with a leafy three-lobed bract

25m (mature)

10m (10 years)

4m (5 years)

Hornbeam

Carpinus betulus

Hornbeams are native trees found largely in south-eastern England, with scattered trees in other parts of the country. It tolerates a wide range of soils, including sands, gravels and heavy clay, but grows best on damp, fertile soils. Hornbeams produce excellent autumn colours, retaining their leaves throughout much of the winter.

One of the hardest and toughest woods in Britain, the name hornbeam derives from the fact that the wood is as hard as horn. It was used for cattle yokes, waterwheels and butchers' chopping blocks. The timber also makes excellent firewood.

Hornbeams are also valuable to wildlife, producing nutlets which are eaten by hawfinches and small mammals. Over 50 species of invertebrates have been found feeding on it.

Seed guide

Hornbeam fruits are a very unusual shape. Each heart-shaped fruit is attached to a leafy three-lobed structure known as a bract, which assists wind dispersal. Collect the fruits by hand from the tree after the bracts have turned brown. Stratify the seeds, usually for one winter. Select and sow germinating seeds in spring.

Did you know?

Hornbeam wood is hard, heavy and tough but was little used in England except as fuel, burning slowly and making the best of charcoal. This led to its wide use in the bread-making industry where it was the perfect fuel for the ovens.

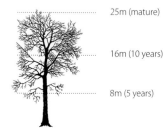

25m (mature)

16m (10 years)

8m (5 years)

Roble Beech

Nothofagus obliqua

This tall deciduous tree reaches heights of 50m in its native Chile, but rarely makes half this height in Britain. The species was introduced to Britain in 1849 by William Lobb. It was grown in Veitch Nurseries in Exeter, although none of the original trees appear to have survived. Reintroduced at the beginning of the 20th century, many of these trees are growing well.

Thought by early explorers to be related to the common beech, they have subsequently been put in their own family – *Nothofagus*, or false beech. Like the common beech, however, this species turns a beautiful yellow or red in the autumn.

Although the roble beech prefers well-drained loamy soil, it can grow on many soils, including sandy ones, but dislikes strongly acid or alkaline soils.

Seed guide

Check the first fall of nuts in autumn – they may be empty. Collect only plump, ripe nuts from the ground. Stratify the seeds for one winter. Select and sow germinating seeds in spring.

Did you know?

'Roble' is Spanish for 'oak', due to the early explorers thinking it was a species of oak.

The Plantswoman's Tale

When Jane Plant popped into her library one day in 1992, she discovered something that was right up her street. Literally. There was a notice attached to the announcement board that caught her eye. Become a Tree Warden, it said, in a nutshell. Help us do something about the trees in our streets. Being a landscape architect, and interested in the design of outdoor spaces, and the ways in which trees can be used to improve any environment, Jane signed up.

Today, Jane is coordinator of the Tree Warden network in the London Borough of Merton. 'We're lucky with Merton Council,' she says, 'in that the relevant officers have a genuine commitment to trees. In addition to the manager of street trees, there are two tree officers in the planning department, as well as the arboricultural manager in the leisure department. Tree Wardens can't get much done if they don't have support from their council. It's a cooperative affair.'

Maintenance plays a big role in Merton's Tree Wardens' lives. The 20 men and women who play an active role in the scheme have a particular battle with self-sown sycamore, which seems to be getting everywhere, crowding out many other more varied species. There's coppicing, tree planting, and commenting on planning applications to be done, as well as regular meetings with council officers, liaisons with other groups, fundraising... All in all, a lot to manage.

'As I'm a freelancer, it's a role I'm able to handle, as I can juggle my work and Tree Warden commitments without worrying about the nine to five structure. It's quite a workload, but it's worth it, because our work is valued by the council, and I can see what we've achieved. Tree Wardens really do make a difference, and I think The Tree Council has developed a good approach with the scheme.'

Over to you

If you too would like to become a volunteer Tree Warden, turn to page 246 for more information.

Large alternate leaves. The seed is attached to a white 'fluff' which helps with wind dispersal

25m (mature)

20m (10 years)

6m (5 years)

Black Poplar

Populus nigra

A native species, this large deciduous tree can grow to 25m. Old trees have deeply furrowed bark, often with large burrs. Black poplar is not a woodland tree, preferring wet edges and stream sides. Country people relied on this tree for fuel-wood, shelter and low-grade timber when no other was available. Male and female trees are identified by the colour and shape of the flowers, males having red catkins and females greenish flowers.

The native form of black poplar is called *Populus nigra* subsp. *betulifolia*. These are beautiful trees but nationally rare, with a current British population of approximately 10,000. Only around 500 of these are females. One parish in Roydon, Essex, has 30 of these, making it probably the finest collection of female trees in Britain.

Roydon's first native black poplar was identified during a Tree Council campaign in 1995, when there were only 1,500 black poplar trees known in the rest of the country.

Seed guide

Usually grown largely from cuttings as there are so few female trees, and hence little seed. However, black poplar can be grown from seed, but it must be sown as soon as it is ripe in spring. Unfortunately, its seeds have an extremely short period of viability and must be sown within a few days of ripening. Sow the seeds on the surface of a pot or seedbed and cover with a thin layer of soil.

Did you know?

In some parts of the country the red male flowers are known as the 'devil's toenails'.

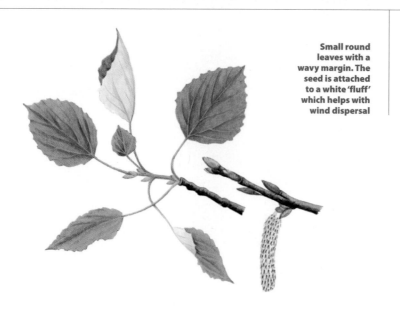

Small round leaves with a wavy margin. The seed is attached to a white 'fluff' which helps with wind dispersal

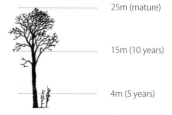

25m (mature)

15m (10 years)

4m (5 years)

Aspen

Populus tremula

A native species of poplar, which can grow to 25m, aspen is found throughout Britain, being most common in Scotland. It prefers cooler climes and is at home in the Highlands, where it often grows side by side with Scots pine and birch.

The leaf stalk (petiole) is flattened, which causes the leaves to tremble in the wind, producing a beautiful sound similar to the crash of waves on a beach. The tree's Latin name, *tremula*, is derived from these trembling leaves. The leaves turn a bright, butter-yellow shade in the autumn, which is another of the tree's notable attributes.

Aspen, like most poplars, are not long-lived – individual trees seldom survive for more than a century. However, it has a remarkable and highly successful method of regeneration through suckers which emerge from the extensive root system, surrounding the 'mother' tree in an ever-extending ring of clonal shoots.

This tree tolerates heavy, cold damp soil but prefers a deep rich well-drained one.

Seed guide

Usually grown largely from cuttings. However, aspen can be grown from seed, but it must be sown as soon as it is ripe in spring. Unfortunately, aspen seeds have an extremely short period of viability and must be sown within a few days of ripening. Sow the seeds on the surface of a pot or seedbed and cover with a thin layer of soil.

Did you know?

Because of its reproduction system, it is thought that the aspen may reach ages of up to 10,000 years old and may be one of the oldest living organisms on Earth. One aspen in the Wasatch Mountains, Utah, USA, is thought to cover an area of 43ha, growing originally from a single rootstock.

And in a similar vein...

There are several other poplars for you to try

Lombardy poplar

Grey poplar

(R) White poplar

Leaves are long with forward-pointing teeth. The leaf stalks have red warts near the leaf. The fruit is a bright red cherry

25m (mature)

18m (10 years)

4m (5 years)

Wild Cherry

Prunus avium

This fast-growing native tree is common in woodlands and has often been planted in parks, gardens and streets for its spring flowers. It prefers deep moist soils, particularly lime-rich ones, but it can grow in fairly acid soils.

Its fine textured wood is used for veneers, musical instruments and cabinet making and was extensively used for making smokers' pipes. It makes good firewood when green, producing perfumed smoke.

Historically the leaves were also used to flavour liquors and custards, while the bark produced a fine yellow dye. At Ely in Cambridgeshire, when the cherries were ripe, people visited the cherry orchards on what was called Cherry Sunday. Arriving at the orchard they paid 6d each, and were then allowed to eat as many cherries as they liked straight from the trees.

Seed guide

Collect the fruits from the tree by hand when they turn yellow-red in July. You may need to collect the seeds before they ripen, otherwise the birds will eat them. Carefully remove the seeds from the flesh and wash thoroughly. Stratify the seeds, usually for one winter. With later collections, germination can be improved by keeping stratifying seeds at room temperature for two weeks, before putting them outside for the winter. Select and sow germinating seeds in spring.

Did you know?

Eaten by humans for many thousands of years, the stones of wild cherry have been found in Bronze Age archaeological sites.

The leaves are almost stalkless. The acorns have long stalks

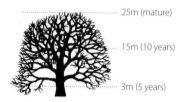

25m (mature)

15m (10 years)

3m (5 years)

English Oak

Quercus robur

The English oak is a native tree of woodlands, hedgerows and parkland in many parts of Britain. It grows best on deep fertile clays and loams but will tolerate a wide range of soils. Some of the largest oaks in Britain are thought to be over 1,000 years old.

The oak has always been the most widely used hardwood in Britain, and its hard, durable timber has traditionally been used for buildings, ships, furniture, panelling and coffins.

The English oak supports 500 species of invertebrates – more than any other species of British tree. The purple hairstreak butterfly breeds solely on this and other species of oak, and small groups of them can often be seen fluttering over the treetops in mid-July to late August. The oak is also used by birds and bats as roosting and nesting sites.

Seed guide

Collect the acorns from the tree, or as soon as possible after they drop – usually from late September onwards. The first to fall should be avoided, as they are often diseased or deformed and unlikely to grow. Take the nuts out of the casing, float them and only plant the ones that sink. To avoid your acorns drying out – which will kill them – sow straight away in a seedbed to a depth of 2-3cm, or singly in pots, covered by a thin layer of compost. Protect throughout the winter. Roots will grow during winter and the shoots will emerge in late April.

Did you know?

Jays love acorns, and hide them away for the winter, giving them an important role in the tree's distribution.

The leaves are composed of 11-15 leaflets, with spines at their tips. The brown or black pea-like pods contain small black seeds

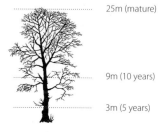

25m (mature)

9m (10 years)

3m (5 years)

False Acacia

Robinia pseudoacacia

Another medium-sized deciduous tree of the pea family, false acacia can reach up to 25m. The species is a native of the east coast of the United States and was introduced into Britain sometime in the 17th century.

A fast-growing tree, it can begin flowering after just six years. The white pea-like flowers hang in scented clusters towards the ends of the branches. The flowers are fragrant and are regularly visited by bees.

A variety of this tree, 'Frisia' – the golden acacia – is widely planted in many gardens and parks throughout the country. Unfortunately, the branches are quite brittle and liable to wind damage.

The small black kidney-shaped seeds are found in brown pods, which can be seen hanging on the tree all winter.

False acacia grows well in any well-drained soil, tolerating drought and atmospheric pollution.

Seed guide

Collect the seed pods from the tree throughout the winter. Split the seeds from the seed pods and store them in a paper bag for the winter. In March puncture the hard, water-impermeable seed coat with a file or knife, without damaging the embryo within. Alternatively, cover the seeds in about five times their volume of boiling water and allow to cool for 12 hours. Sow chipped or swollen seeds in an outdoor seedbed in March or April.

Did you know?

The first half of the plant's Latin name is in honour of Jean Robin, the French gardener who received seeds from America in 1601.

25m (mature)
20m (10 years)

6m (5 years)

White Willow

Salix alba

This deciduous native tree, with upright, ascending branches, can reach a height of 25m. Like many willows, this species grows quickly, and the name 'white willow' comes from the fact that the young leaves are covered with whitish silky hairs on both surfaces. These appear only on the lower surface as the leaf gets older.

The flowers appear at the same time as the leaves and, when fertilised, comprise numerous small capsules containing tiny seeds surrounded by white 'down', which aids dispersal of the seeds in the wind.

There are many types of white willow, the most famous of which is the cricket bat willow, a tree discovered in Norfolk in about 1700 and considered to be the perfect tree for the production of cricket bats.

Preferring wet soils, this species does badly on thin soils like chalk. Like the black poplar, it is probably only suitable for large gardens, but a good species for river edges and wet woodlands.

Seed guide

Because this species is easy to grow from cuttings, it is not often grown from seed. However, this is possible, although it must be sown as soon as it is ripe in spring. Unfortunately, white willow seeds have an extremely short period of viability and must be sown within a few days of ripening. Sow the seeds on the surface of a pot or seedbed and cover with a thin layer of soil.

Did you know?

The bark of this tree produces a chemical called salicin, which was used in the development of aspirin.

And in a similar vein...

There are several other willows for you to try

Weeping willow

Crack willow   (R) White willow

Long pinnate leaves with 15 leaflet pairs. The long pea-like fruits contain brown/yellow seeds

25m (mature)

9m (10 years)

3m (5 years)

Pagoda Tree

Sophora japonica

This is a large deciduous tree, which can reach a height of 25m. Despite the name *japonica*, it is only found naturally in China and was introduced to Britain in 1753 by James Gordon, a celebrated nurseryman of Mile End, London.

Another member of the pea family, this tree has white/yellow flowers in large groups at the ends of its branches, although in Britain the trees can take up to 40 years before they first flower. In Britain the tree flowers late in the season, in August, September and even October, but seldom fruits.

The seed pods, when they are produced, are long and contain one to five kidney-shaped, dark brown seeds.

Extensively used in China for medicinal purposes, the flowers, fruit, bark and root have been used for centuries. The wood is tough and durable but when fresh contains chemicals which can cause medical problems.

The plant prefers well-drained sandy, loamy or heavy clay soils, but cannot grow in the shade.

Seed guide

Collect the ripe seed pods from the tree before the pods burst. Store for the winter in a paper bag. In March puncture the hard, water-impermeable seed coat with a file or knife, without damaging the embryo within. Alternatively, cover the seeds in about five times their volume of boiling water and allow to cool for 12 hours. Sow chipped or swollen seeds in an outdoor seedbed in March or April.

Did you know?

The pagoda tree was planted in Chinese cemeteries to mark the graves of officials of 'low degree'.

The shiny lobed leaves have their basal lobes at right angles to the leaf stalk. The rounded brown fruit is found in clusters

25m (mature)

10m (10 years)

3m (5 years)

Wild Service Tree

Sorbus torminalis

The wild service tree is the rarer woodland relative of rowan and whitebeam, appearing to germinate only in areas of ancient woodland, for which it is an indicator. It is found mainly on chalk and limestone but also on nutrient-rich clays. It has spectacular autumn colour.

Its hard fine-grained wood has been used as a veneer, while the berries were eaten to cure colic. In the Weald of Kent and Sussex, wild service fruit is known as 'chequers' or 'chequer berries'. There are many pubs in this area called The Chequers, and it may be that a drink was made from the berries or that they were added to beer.

Wild service berries provide good food for birds.

Seed guide

Warning – wild service trees are prone to interbreed with many other *Sorbus* species, so the seeds may not be true wild service trees.

The fully ripe clusters of berries should be picked from the tree in September. Carefully remove the seeds from the flesh and wash thoroughly. Stratify the seeds, usually for one winter. In cool autumns, germination can be improved by keeping stratifying seeds at room temperature for two weeks, before putting them outside for the winter. Select and sow germinating seeds in spring.

Did you know?

The fruit of this tree has been made into a beer, although it does have an odd taste.

The leaves are dark green with tufts of orange hairs at the vein junctions on the underside. The fruits are not ribbed or hairy

25m (mature)

12m (10 years)

3m (5 years)

Small-leaved Lime

Tilia cordata

The small-leaved lime is an uncommon but attractive native species. It is found as woodland in Worcestershire and East Anglia, and naturally occurring individual trees can be found in woodland as far north as Cumbria. The tree is long-lived and some specimens are thought to be 2,000 years old.

In Roman times it was known as 'the tree of a thousand uses'. The wood is soft and was used in carving, woodturning, model making and for making keys for pianos and organs. The best known carver of lime was Grinling Gibbons (1648-1721), whose work decorates churches and stately homes.

The tree has considerable wildlife value, with the flowers attracting insects, particularly bees. Lime honey is highly prized across Europe.

Small-leaved lime prefers a moist loamy alkaline to neutral soil but will grow on slightly acid soils. It grows poorly on any very dry or very wet soil. The species tolerates considerable exposure and succeeds in sun or semi-shade.

Seed guide

Lime fruits are a very unusual shape. The clusters of round fruits are attached via stalks to a single, leaf-like bract, which assists wind dispersal. Collect the fruits by hand from the tree after the bracts have turned brown, usually following a frost. Stratify the seeds for one or two winters. Select and sow germinating seeds in spring.

Did you know?

A form of woven rope was made from the under or inner bark (bast) of the small-leaved lime.

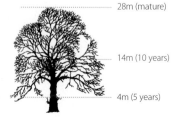

The distinctive hand-shaped leaf has five to seven leaflets. The seeds are shiny brown conkers

28m (mature)

14m (10 years)

4m (5 years)

Horse Chestnut

Aesculus hippocastanum

The horse chestnut, which was introduced into Britain from the Balkans in the early 17th century, is now commonly found on village greens and in streets, parks and gardens. It tolerates a wide range of conditions, including dry sandy soils, wet clays and chalk, but prefers moist well-drained soils.

Its weak wood is not widely used but its absorbent properties make it ideal for fruit racks and storage trays, as it keeps the fruit dry and so prevents rotting. Its familiar fruit – the conker – is well known to most schoolchildren.

As to the wildlife value of the tree, its nuts provide food for deer and other mammals and its flowers provide pollen for insects. A moth pest species – the horse chestnut leaf miner moth – has recently arrived in the UK. The moth's caterpillars eat the chlorophyll from within the leaves, leaving brown spots and reducing the tree's health. The long-term effect of this is currently unknown.

Seed guide

Collect plump, ripe, healthy-looking nuts from the ground in autumn. Take the nuts out of the spiky casing, float them and only plant the ones that sink. Sow immediately in a pot or seedbed; protect from predators and severe frost.

Did you know?

Each year there is a World Conker Championship in Ashton, Northamptonshire on the second Sunday in October.

And in a similar vein…

There are several other horse chestnuts for you to try

Ohio buckeye

Sweet buckeye

(R) Indian horse chestnut 'Sydney Pearce'

The Storyteller's Tale

'I've been interested in trees since I was a child,' says Irena Krasinska-Lobban, 'and it had a lot to do with my grandfather. He was a dour Highlander, and a master storyteller. He'd link tales to the trees – I remember, for example, that he'd tell that you can recognise a beech tree because it has fairy houses beneath it.'

Irena has inherited her grandfather's love of stories, and of trees. Since her return to Perthshire she's been an active Tree Warden. 'It's so important to protect trees,' she says, 'because they can't speak for themselves. They're special in so many ways. Up the road from where I live, for example, is Niel Gow's Oak, as it's known. Back in the 18th century he was one of Scotland's finest ever fiddlers, and he wrote so much of his music sitting under that tree.'

But trees aren't just notable for their famous connections. They have roles to play in all our lives. 'Take for example the "swing tree",' says Irena. 'When I was young, my friends and I used to use it to hang ropes from and swing across a burn. We all called it the "swing tree", and later generations probably know it by that name, too. There are "swing trees", and other appellations, all over the country, because there are so many trees that mean something to someone.'

Yet it's not just about keeping old trees. 'We need young trees, too, which will become the basis of stories for the future,' she says.

In her role as Tree Warden, Irena helps take care of a community woodland near Perth, and sows as many seeds, such as acorns, as she can. 'I have hope for the future of trees, because we're aware of the overall damage to the environment we're causing, and being aware is the first step to doing something about it.'

Over to you

If you too would like to become a volunteer Tree Warden, turn to page 246 for more information.

The alternate leaves have on their underside tufts of orange hairs at the junctions of the veins. The female fruit is a green cone which turns black after the seed is shed

30m (mature)

20m (10 years)

8m (5 years)

Italian Alder

Alnus cordata

This conical-shaped deciduous tree can grow to 30m. It has a very restricted natural distribution, being confined to Corsica and southern Italy, and was brought to the UK in the 1820s.

The heart-shaped leaves and overall shape of the tree mean that it can be confused with the wild pear – but look for the distinctive cone-like fruits at the ends of the branches. As with common alder, these cones and the immature male catkins hang on the tree all winter, making them easy to spot.

Unlike other alders, Italian alder thrives on dry and poor soils, which has made it an ideal tree for planting on difficult sites, such as spoil heaps, roadside schemes and other urban regeneration projects.

The wood of all alders is very durable, especially in water, and it has been suggested that Italian alder was used for the wooden piles upon which the city of Venice is built. However, as most of the wood for the piles was brought from Slovenia, it is more likely to be common alder.

Seed guide

Alder cones can be collected from the lower branches of trees before they open from September onwards. Place cones in a paper bag and allow to air-dry at room temperature. As the cones open they will release their tiny seeds, which often contain a high percentage that are empty. Don't bother trying to separate them! The tiny seeds can be sown immediately and should be covered by a thin layer of sharp sand, and left over winter until they germinate the following spring.

Did you know?

A useful identification tip is that the ripe yellow male catkins are significantly larger than those of the common alder.

These leaves have hairy stalks and triangular bases. The teeth on the edges of these leaves are more regular than on silver birch. The fruiting catkins stay on the tree until winter

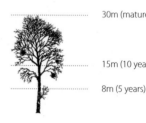

30m (mature)

15m (10 years)

8m (5 years)

Downy Birch

Betula pubescens

The native downy birch prefers wetter conditions than silver birch and is most widespread in the north and west of Britain, on poorly drained soils. Its bark is often darker than the silver birch, particularly at its base.

The wood of this tree was used to make furniture and veneers, while the branches were used to make besom brooms. The sugary sap, drawn from this and the silver birch, is used to produce birch wine, while oils from the bark can be used as an insect repellent.

As with silver birch, downy birch is excellent for wildlife and again provides food for birds including black grouse, which can sometimes be seen feeding on the young catkins. Up to 334 invertebrate species have been recorded in birches.

Seed guide

Birch cones can be collected from the lower branches of trees. Place the cones in a paper bag and allow them to dry at room temperature. Ripe cones will disintegrate on drying, leaving a mixture of tiny winged seeds, plus *fleur-de-lys*-shaped bracts. Don't bother trying to separate them! The tiny seeds can be sown immediately and should be covered by a thin layer of sharp sand, and left over winter until they germinate the following spring.

Did you know?

Downy birch grows well in northern latitudes and can be found in Greenland and Iceland, becoming the tallest native tree in these harsh climates.

And in a similar vein...

There are several other birches for you to try

Chinese red birch

River birch

(R) Japanese white birch

Large spear-shaped leaves with saw-toothed edges. The glossy brown nuts are encased in a spiny green case

30m (mature)

20m (10 years)

5m (5 years)

Sweet Chestnut

Castanea sativa

The sweet chestnut was probably introduced to Britain from the Mediterranean by the Romans, who had a liking for chestnuts. The species is now widely established in Britain, being actively managed as coppiced woodland, especially in the south. The species prefers deep, moist sandy soils and drained clays, but doesn't do well on very wet or lime-rich soils.

The strong, tough wood is good for fence posts and props and the chestnuts are edible when roasted.

The tree provides good nest sites for woodpeckers and nuthatches, while nightingales often live in coppiced sweet chestnut woodlands.

The oldest sweet chestnut in the country is the famous Tortworth Chestnut, an amazing tree which is thought to be over 1,200 years old. This ancient hulk looks more like a small woodland rather than an individual tree.

Seed guide

Collect plump, ripe, healthy-looking nuts from the ground in autumn. Take the nuts out of the spiky casing, float them and only plant the ones that sink. Sow immediately in a pot or seedbed; protect from predators and severe frost.

Did you know?

The edible sweet chestnut nuts have been cultivated since at least Roman times. Chestnuts are rich in carbohydrates, providing a source of quickly digestible energy, resulting in a wide range of culinary uses, from baked chestnuts and jams to puddings and stuffing.

30m (mature)

22m (10 years)

4m (5 years)

Cider Gum

Eucalyptus gunnii

A tall tree, reaching heights of 30m, this species is a native of Tasmania. It was discovered by Sir J Hooker in 1840 and was introduced to Britain shortly after its discovery.

It has very distinctive young foliage, which is round and stalkless. As the tree gets beyond four years, the leaves become long and willow-like. This does cause some problems in British gardens, because the young trees are often sold for their juvenile foliage without the owners realising that the mature tree can be of considerable size. This they can achieve in a relatively short time, as the species can make up to 2m growth in a year.

The clusters of small flowers appear late in the year and can provide a useful late source of nectar for bees, before the onset of winter.

Cider gum tolerates poor soils, but prefers a sunny position in a fertile moisture-retentive soil. It is very frost resistant.

Seed guide

The small fruits are cup-shaped and contain minute seeds. These should be collected and stored in a paper bag until the early spring, when they can be sown directly onto the surface of the soil, either in pots or a seedbed.

Did you know?

Often purchased for its juvenile foliage, the leaves change from small and round to long and pointed, as the tree grows rapidly.

And in a similar vein...

There are several other eucalyptuses for you to try

Alpine ash

Spinning gum

(R) Bogong gum

The leaves have nine to 13 pairs of stalked leaflets, with a single terminal leaflet. The single seeds have a long wing

30m (mature)

15m (10 years)

3m (5 years)

Ash

Fraxinus excelsior

The ash is a very widespread woodland native tree growing throughout Britain, preferring moist, well-drained and fertile soils. Large, spreading ash trees can often be seen in hedgerows but, as it lacks much autumn colour, it is now infrequently planted in parks and gardens. A mature ash can produce 100,000 seeds.

Its strong wood is flexible and was used as an element in wheel making, for skis, oars and tool handles. It is still used for high-quality furniture.

It is a species with a high wildlife value, as it is used as a nesting site by woodpeckers and other hole-nesters, including redstarts. The tree also supports up to 68 species of invertebrates and over 200 species of lichen.

Ash prefers a deep loamy soil, but can succeed in very exposed positions, including coastal conditions, although they may become wind-blown. Can grow on alkaline soils but not in shallow soils over chalk. Very intolerant of shade, young trees fail to grow in dense-shade areas.

Seed guide

Clusters of ash fruits are known as keys. Wait until they have turned brown before collecting them from the tree. Separate the individual keys and stratify for at least two winters. Protect from predators and severe frost. Select and sow germinating seeds in early spring of the second and successive years.

Did you know?

The tree's flowers may be male, female or hermaphrodite. The flowers open before the leaves, and while both male and female flowers can occur on the same tree, it is common to find all male and all female trees. Surprisingly, however, a tree that is all male one year can produce female flowers the next, and similarly a female tree can become male. How this happens is still unknown.

And in a similar vein…

There are several other ashes for you to try

Fraxinus sieboldiana

Manna ash

(R) White ash

Unique fan-shaped leaves with two lobes. The fruits are orange when ripe and contain seeds

30m (mature)

5m (10 years)
2m (5 years)

Maidenhair Tree

Ginkgo biloba

Ginkgo are large trees which can reach 30m tall. When young, the tree has a pyramidal shape, becoming broader and more spreading as it grows older.

Ginkgo trees are the only survivors of a group of plants (*Ginkgoales*) which were widespread 190 million years ago. Thought by some scientists to be the first trees to have evolved, they grew in Britain 60 million years ago. Fossil remains can still be found in Scarborough. About 30 million years ago the species formed stands across the London basin but then disappeared as a result of climatic changes.

Ginkgos were brought back to Europe from Japan during the 18th century and arrived in Britain in 1754.

The unique leaves are very distinctive, and the male and female trees are separate. The males are more pyramidal and upright in habit, while the females are more compact.

They thrive in deep, well-drained, rich soil and are excellent trees for towns and cities, as they are resistant to attack by insects and fungi and the leaves resist the smoke of cities.

Seed guide

Collect the bright orange, fleshy fruits once they are ripe. Remove the seeds from the flesh and wash them thoroughly. Stratify the seeds, usually for one winter. Select and sow germinating seeds next spring.

Did you know?

Ancient ginkgos produce strange nodular aerial roots, which hang from the underside of branches. In Japan these are known as *chichi* which is Japanese for 'breast'.

Each large leaf has seven leaflets which get larger towards the tip. The round green fruit contains the familiar wrinkled brown nut

30m (mature)

10m (10 years)

3m (5 years)

Walnut

Juglans regia

The walnut was probably introduced into Britain by the Romans and has subsequently become widespread in southern and central England, especially in hedgerows. Further north it is found largely in parks and gardens. The tree grows best on moderately fertile, well-drained soils and will grow on chalky soils. It dislikes wet or shallow soils, or peat.

Often called the 'king of timbers', this hardwood was used to make aeroplane propellers and is still used for cabinet making, decorative veneer and rifle butts.

The foliage of walnut gives off a scent similar to shoe polish and a sprig kept in a jar is said to deter flies. The walnut itself is widely eaten by humans, either pickled or raw. Rooks also like them and many trees grow from walnuts buried and forgotten by these birds.

Seed guide

Collect the fruits from the tree or ground as soon as the husks darken or turn black. Remove the husks and sow immediately in a pot or seedbed; protect from predators and severe frost.

Did you know?

An ink can be made from the green husks surrounding the walnut by simmering them in water. The ink produced is a warm brown colour, which darkens as it dries out.

Five-lobed leaves which are alternate, unlike the five-lobed maple leaves which are opposite. The spiky fruits contain smaller winged brown seeds

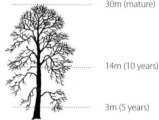

30m (mature)

14m (10 years)

3m (5 years)

Sweet Gum

Liquidambar styraciflua

A large deciduous tree which can reach heights of 50m in its native America, but rarely makes more than 30m in the UK. It is another tree first grown at the Palace Gardens by Bishop Compton at Fulham in 1681.

The fruits are round and spiky, and are composed of numerous capsules (20-50), each capsule containing one to two small seeds, although often only a few are fertile. The bright green leaves turn a brilliant red-purple or yellow colour in the autumn, making this an excellent tree for parks and large gardens. However, the wood is brittle, which can lead to branches dropping off in high winds.

The tree can exude a resin, known as liquid amber, which can be clear, reddish or yellow, with a pleasant smell. This resin hardens into a solid form which, historically, was shipped around the world in barrels. It was used in France as a perfume.

Sweet gum prefers a moist but not swampy soil in a sunny sheltered position, disliking shallow soils overlying chalk.

Seed guide

Collect the fruit as it ripens at the end of October or November. Take it from the tree before it splits, put it into a paper bag and keep in a warm room. Shake the bag until the seeds fall out of the capsules. The seeds require one to three months' stratification and sometimes take two years to germinate. Once germinated, sow in the early spring into pots or a seedbed.

Did you know?

In California the spiky seed cases are called 'ankle twisters', as they make it difficult to walk beneath the trees after they have seeded.

Unusual four-lobed leaves with a flattened end. The cone-shaped fruits contain the smaller seeds

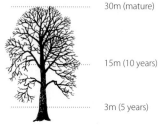

30m (mature)

15m (10 years)

3m (5 years)

Tulip Tree

Liriodendron tulipifera

A tall tree reaching a height of 30m, this native of the east coast of the United States was probably introduced to Britain in the middle of the 17th century by John Tradescant.

A member of the magnolia family, the tree has magnolia-like flowers, but very different buds and twigs. The leaves have a distinctive shape, looking as though the end has been cut off. In autumn they turn bright yellow-gold in colour, making the tree very attractive at this time of year. The fruit is found in a cone-like structure, inside which the light brown seeds develop.

The timber of the tulip tree is used in North America for many purposes, and is also largely imported to England under the name of canary wood.

The tree requires a deep, moist, rich soil, preferring it to be slightly acid. It grows well in both sun and semi-shade.

Seed guide

Collect the seeds from October onwards once the fruit turns brown. Stratify the seeds for seven to 12 weeks outdoors. Germination is usually poor – only about one per cent of the seed is viable. Take the germinating seeds and pot up in a pot or a seedbed.

Did you know?

The tulip tree is a major honey plant in its native areas, producing a strong reddish honey.

The leaves feel rough to the touch and the twigs have hairy buds. The acorn cups also have coarse bristles

30m (mature)

16m (10 years)

4m (5 years)

Turkey Oak

Quercus cerris

The turkey oak is a tree introduced from southern Europe. It appears to have been brought to Britain by a Devon nurseryman called Lucombe in the early 18th century.

Turkey oaks grow on light soils as far north as Scotland and are often planted in parks and gardens. The tree seeds freely and has therefore become widely naturalised.

The wood of turkey oak is of poor quality. If used outdoors it splits easily, so it has been used largely for panelling and other interior decorations.

Turkey oaks play host to a species of *Cynipid* gall wasp, which destroys English and sessile oak acorns. Turkey oaks should, therefore, only be planted very selectively.

Seed guide

Collect the acorns from the tree or as soon as possible after they drop – usually from October onwards. Take the nuts out of the spiky casing, float them and only plant the ones that sink. Do not let the acorns dry out, or they will die. Sow straight away in a seedbed to a depth of 2-3cm, or singly in pots, covered with a thin layer of compost. Protect from predators throughout the winter. Roots will emerge during the winter and the shoots in late April.

Did you know?

The *Cynipid* wasp that lives on turkey oak is *Andricus quercuscalicis*. If it lays its eggs in English or sessile acorns they form distinctive knopper galls. The word knopper derives from 'knop' – a small rounded protuberance.

The leaves have distinct stalks. The acorns are without stalks, hence the name 'sessile' (unstalked)

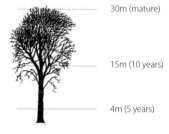

30m (mature)

15m (10 years)

4m (5 years)

Sessile Oak

Quercus petraea

The large sessile oak is a native tree of woodlands and hedgerows in the west of Britain. It prefers areas of high rainfall and grows best in deep, well-drained clays and loams. Like English oak, some of the largest trees may be over 1,000 years old.

Its hard durable timber is used for boats, buildings and furniture.

The branches of sessile oak are not too closely spaced, which allows light to reach the forest floor. This ensures that sessile oak woodland has a good ground flora, but also allows a wide range of insects and birds to feed in the spaces between the trees. Pied flycatchers and redstarts are just two examples of the birds which thrive in woods of this species.

Seed guide

Collect the acorns from the tree, or as soon as possible after they drop – usually from late September onwards. Take the nuts out of the casing, float them and only plant the ones that sink. Do not let the acorns dry out, or they will die. Sow straight away in a seedbed to a depth of 2-3cm, or singly in pots, covered by a thin layer of compost. Protect from predators throughout the winter. Roots will emerge during the winter and the shoots in late April.

Did you know?

The leaves of English oaks have short 5mm stalks and basal ear-like lobes (auricles). The acorns are stalked, with up to four on each. Pure sessile oaks have larger leaves, with 10-20mm stalks and no lobes. The acorns are stalkless.

The evergreen leaves are alternate with triangular, pointed lobes. The acorns sit in a hairy acorn cup

30m (mature)

16m (10 years)

4m (5 years)

Lucombe Oak

Quercus x *hispanica*

These large evergreen oaks (up to 30m) are a natural hybrid between cork oak (*Quercus suber*) and turkey oak (*Quercus cerris*). The nature of the hybrids is variable and the trees can exhibit a variety of characteristics of both parents.

The tree takes its name from William Lucombe, who grew a number of seedlings in his nursery in Exeter around 1762. The hybrid between the species is frequent in the wild in south-west Europe and can be found growing in Britain, particularly in the south-west where it originated.

The tree grows well in fertile loamy soils and can tolerate shade.

Seed guide

Collect the acorns from the tree or soon after they drop – usually from October. Take the nuts out of the casing, float them and only plant those that sink. Do not let them dry out. Sow in a seedbed to a depth of 2-3cm, or singly in pots, covered with a thin layer of compost. Protect through the winter. Roots will emerge during winter and the shoots in late April. As it's a hybrid, the seeds will not produce a tree identical to the parent.

Did you know?

The original tree was felled by Mr Lucombe for his own coffin. He stored the timber under his bed, but then lived much longer than he thought he would (102 years old), so he had a larger tree cut down and stored these new boards under his bed until they were eventually needed.

And in a similar vein...

There are other oaks for you to try

Red oak

Chestnut-leaved oak

(R) Holm oak

The Council Officer's Tale

Some people are Tree Wardens who work with the council, while some are council officers who work with Tree Wardens. Nicola Williams (right), unusually, is both. A Tree Warden for more than 15 years, she's also Basingstoke and Deane Borough Council's arboricultural officer.

'I've always been interested in trees, ever since I grew up on a farm in Hampshire,' she says. 'Being a Tree Warden – and there are 40 of us – is very rewarding in Basingstoke, partly because the council has a very enlightened outlook here. It's very supportive of volunteer organisations, so when the opportunity came up to apply for a council role, I was keen to do so.'

To strengthen the borough's resolve, the council has put together a tree policy which sets out the important contribution of trees to the environment. 'Yet there's still much work to be done,' says Nicola. 'As a Tree Warden and a council officer, I believe that education has a very important role to play in improving the prospect for trees and the wider environment. Fly-tipping, for example, is one of those things that few people fully understand. We all know that you shouldn't leave your rubbish by the

side of a wood, but many don't realise that you also shouldn't tip green waste, such as lawn cuttings, either. There is, I believe, a growing understanding of the importance of trees, but what we have to do, nationally, is encourage and educate people on how to protect them.'

One of the buzzes Nicola gets comes from walking around Basingstoke and seeing the trees that she and her colleagues planted, growing tall and strong. 'For an urban landscape, the town really is very green,' she says. 'From the beautiful copper beeches in the War Memorial Park, to the old great beech on the Harrow Way, Basingstoke is a good example of what can be achieved.'

Over to you

If you too would like to become a volunteer Tree Warden, turn to page 246 for more information.

The rough hairy leaves have an unequal base and strong teeth around the margin. The leaves also turn a distinctive yellow in autumn. The seed is set in the centre of the fruit

30m (mature)

16m (10 years)

4m (5 years)

Wych Elm

Ulmus glabra

The native wych elm is commonly found in hillside woods in Scotland, but is much less common in the south of Britain. Like other elms, this species has suffered from Dutch elm disease and its population is much reduced. It prefers growing on heavy moist clays and loams but will grow on chalk soils.

The fact that its wood is tough, even when wet, led to its use in making boats and for underground water pipes. Like other elms, it was also used to make wheel hubs, as the wood resists splitting.

White-letter hairstreak butterflies lay their eggs on the wych elm. Up to 81 other species of insect have been recorded on the tree.

Easily grown in any well-drained soil, wych elm is moderately shade tolerant, wind resistant and tolerant of maritime exposure.

Seed guide

Collect the fruits from the tree, when the wings begin to turn brown in May/June. The winged fruits can be sown immediately into seed trays. A small percentage will germinate quite quickly; however many fruits are empty of seed and will never germinate. Keep well watered and shaded in hot weather. Prick out seedlings into final containers. May need to be grown for two years.

Did you know?

'Wych' has its origins in Old English, and means 'pliant' or 'supple'.

Leaves are large and five-lobed, with dark green upper sides. The angle of the seeds is much narrower than field maple

35m (mature)

16m (10 years)

4m (5 years)

Sycamore

Acer pseudoplatanus

This species grows in a wide range of habitats and soil types. Sycamore is an excellent coloniser and is often considered a problem species as in certain habitats, including woodland, it can become the dominant species.

Sycamore wood is light in colour, strong and hard, and is used for kitchen tabletops, flooring, veneers and toys.

Recently, the debate on whether the sycamore is a native or non-native tree has been re-opened. Sycamore is so widely distributed in Britain that only ash and hawthorn are more widespread. Yet its invasive potential, and heavy honeydew production, have given it a poor reputation. However, sycamore produces high-quality timber and provides an important food source for some species of invertebrates (eg bees) and is an important source of food for some migrating birds. Therefore, perhaps the debate over 'natural or not' is irrelevant and the question should be 'is sycamore valuable in the countryside?' To which the answer is probably a cautious 'yes'.

Seed guide

Collect the fruits from the tree in autumn when they turn brown. Do not let the fruits dry out, or they will die. Stratify the seeds for one winter. Select and sow germinating seeds in spring. Alternatively, sow immediately in a pot or seedbed, and allow to stratify naturally over winter. Protect from predators and severe frost.

Did you know?

The sycamore was first written about in England by Henry Lyte in 1578, although there is a carving at Christ Church, Oxford on a shrine to St Frideswide, which includes leaves and seeds of sycamore, and is dated 1289. This suggests that the species has been in Britain longer than people imagine.

The single needles are dark green and in rosettes. The large winged seeds are contained within the cone

35m (mature)

8m (10 years)

2m (5 years)

Cedar of Lebanon

Cedrus libani

This large ornamental tree, growing to a height of 35m, is a native of the mountains of the Mediterranean region, in Turkey, Lebanon and western Syria. The species was probably first brought to Britain as seed by Dr Edward Pococke, a scholar of Arabic at Oxford University, who made several journeys to Syria in 1638-1639. This tree is the national emblem of Lebanon and is on the country's flag. However, due to a long history of felling, few old trees remain in the country, although there are active efforts to conserve the tree.

This beautiful evergreen conifer, can frequently be found in the grounds of Georgian manor houses, as it needs considerable space to grow. Its distinctive profile has flat-topped branches, on top of which sit the tree's cones. These solitary cones are slightly flattened on the top, and contain brown, roughly triangular seeds.

Requiring warm, deep, well-drained soils, cedar of Lebanon grows best in the south and east of the country. Once established it is tolerant of chalk, dry sites and drought.

Seed guide

Collect the cones from the tree when they have turned from green to brown. Keep the cones in a bag or on a dish, at room temperature, to air-dry them. This causes them to disintegrate and release their seeds, which can be sown immediately. Cover with a thin layer of sharp sand and leave over winter to germinate the following spring.

Did you know?

An oil distilled from the wood of the cedar of Lebanon was used in ancient Egypt to embalm the dead.

And in a similar vein...

There are several other cedars for you to try

'Pendulous' cedar of Lebanon

Deodar cedar

(R) Atlantic cedar

35m (mature)

10m (10 years)

4m (5 years)

Beech

Fagus sylvatica

The beech is the dominant native species on chalk and limestone. It prefers well-drained soils but can be found in heavy clays. It has been widely planted in parks and gardens, as well as in hedging, especially in Exmoor. Beech is well known for its excellent autumn colour, but the early 'spring green' of the leaves is also extremely attractive.

The wood is strong and tough and was once used for tool handles and flooring. It is still used for kitchen utensils and children's toys. The beechmast (nuts) make good pig feed, and are widely eaten by mice, squirrels, and birds. Bats like to roost in holes in the stem, or amongst the tangles of exposed roots, if they occur. The dense shade cast by beechwoods means that they have a restricted but specialised flora, including bird's-nest orchid, the rare ghost orchid and various helleborines. Some 94 species of invertebrates have been found in beech trees, including lobster and barred hook-tip moths.

Seed guide

Check the first fall of beechnuts in autumn – they may be empty. Collect only plump, ripe nuts from the ground. Sow immediately in a pot or seedbed; protect from predators and severe frost.

Did you know?

One large beech tree produces, in a year, sufficient oxygen for 10 people.

And in a similar vein...

There are several other beeches for you to try

Copper beech

'Quercifolia' beech

(R) Dawyk beech

Single needles are green and soft, occurring as rosettes on older branches. The small winged seeds are contained within the cone

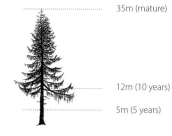

35m (mature)

12m (10 years)

5m (5 years)

European Larch

Larix decidua

This large deciduous conifer can reach heights of 35m. Its native range includes upland areas in the Alps, Russia and Poland, and it was introduced to Britain in the early 17th century. It was grown as an ornamental tree until it was taken to Scotland. The earliest trees in Scotland arrived in 1738, brought by a Mr Menzies, in his portmanteau, five of which he left for James, Duke of Atholl. Of those five, one of the original trees remains standing.

The duke saw the potential of the tree for timber and by 1830 all the dukes of Atholl had planted over 14 million larch trees, covering nearly 4,250ha.

Unlike most conifers larch is deciduous, shedding its leaves each winter and putting out fresh green needles every spring.

The small egg-shaped cones occur all around the branches and remain throughout the winter, the seeds being important for birds such as the redpoll and siskin.

The wood has been used in yacht building because it is tough, durable and flexible.

Seed guide

Cones can be collected from the tree when they have turned from green to brown (October to January). The cones persist on the tree for years, and care must be taken not to collect old, spent cones which have already shed their seeds. Larch seeds often contain a significant proportion of filled, but woody and, therefore, dead seeds. Keep the cones in a bag or on a dish, at room temperature, to air-dry them. This causes them to open and release their seeds, which can be sown immediately. Cover with a thin layer of sharp sand, and leave over winter, to germinate the following spring.

Did you know?

In Scotland the buds and cones are food for the capercaillie.

Large, alternate, five-lobed leaves. The fruit is a peculiar spiky seed ball

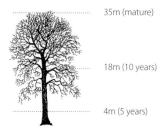

35m (mature)

18m (10 years)

4m (5 years)

London Plane

Platanus x *hispanica*

This large deciduous tree can reach heights of 35m. It is thought to be a hybrid between Oriental (*P. orientalis*) and American plane (*P. occidentalis*), although it may simply be a form of Oriental plane. First noticed about 1663, it may be that the hybrid cross occurred in John Tradescant's garden in Lambeth, as both species were growing there.

The London plane copes well with pollution, and this hybrid was therefore planted widely in urban streets and squares, changing for ever the treescape of British cities. It has a distinctive bark with large plates which flake off, leaving creamy patches. The leaves also show characteristics between the two parent species, being more deeply lobed than American plane and less so than the Oriental. The seed balls are usually in pairs and produce fertile seeds.

The species grows well in moist loamy soil, but can tolerate very wet, poorly drained soils. Established plants are drought tolerant and wind-resistant.

Seed guide

Collect seed balls anytime after they turn brown. Allow to dry at room temperature until the ball can be broken up to release tiny, individual seeds. There is frequently a high percentage that are empty. Don't bother trying to separate them! The tiny seeds can be sown immediately and should be covered by a thin layer of sharp sand, and left over winter until they germinate the following spring.

Did you know?

The leaf of the London plane is the symbol of the New York City Department of Parks and Recreation, and is prominently featured on signs and buildings in public parks across the city.

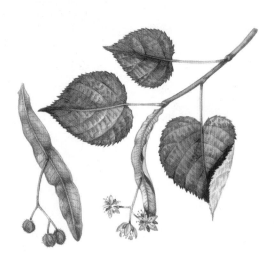

Leaves appear earlier than other limes and are hairy on top, and deeply hairy underneath. The stalk is also hairy. The rounded fruit is five-ribbed, with short hairs

35m (mature)

18m (10 years)

3m (5 years)

Large-leaved Lime

Tilia platyphyllos

The large-leaved lime is a rare native tree, growing on limestone and chalk in the Wye Valley, the Pennines and the South Downs. The species prefers lime-rich soils but will grow on sandy sites and has been used occasionally for town and street tree plantings.

As with the other limes, the wood of this species resists splitting, and so was used for artificial limbs, wooden clogs and toys.

Flowering slightly earlier than other limes, this tree provides early nectar sources for insects. The foliage is very palatable for browsing animals, and many moths use the species, including the spectacular lime hawkmoth.

The species prefers a moist loamy alkaline to neutral soil, but will grow on slightly acid soils. It grows poorly on any very dry or very wet soil. Large-leaved lime tolerates considerable exposure and succeeds in sun or semi-shade.

Seed guide

Lime fruits are a very unusual shape. The clusters of round fruits are attached via stalks to a single, leaf-like bract, which assists wind dispersal. Collect the fruits by hand from the tree after the bracts have turned brown, usually following a frost. Stratify the seeds for one or two winters. Select and sow germinating seeds in spring.

Did you know?

Lime trees are very important to beekeepers as a source of nectar for bees, who produce a very pale but richly flavoured honey, which has a slightly addictive quality to it.

The paired needles are usually twisted. The cones ripen over three years from green to brown, when the seeds are shed

36m (mature)

12m (10 years)

3m (5 years)

Scots Pine

Pinus sylvestris

The Scots pine is the only native pine in Britain. It is found on heathlands in the south of England, but is most widespread in Scotland, where there are extensive stands of old trees, especially in the Spey Valley and Upper Dee areas. It grows on a wide range of soils, but prefers light and dry sands and gravels.

Scots pine produces strong, moderately hard wood that was used for charcoal and telegraph poles, and is still used for doors, floors and furniture.

The tree has excellent wildlife value, with 172 invertebrate species, including the pine hawkmoth, feeding on it. In Scottish pinewoods, it provides nesting sites for ospreys and Scottish crossbills, and the cones provide food for red squirrels which, in turn, are eaten by the rare pine marten.

Scots pine thrives in a light well-drained sandy or gravelly soil. It tolerates chalk, but the trees are usually short-lived, and some water-logging. The species is also wind resistant and tolerates coastal conditions.

Seed guide

Scots pine cones can be collected from the lower branches of trees when they have turned from green to brown (October to January). Keep the cones in a bag or on a dish, at room temperature, to air-dry them. This causes them to open and release their seeds, which can be sown immediately. Cover with a thin layer of sharp sand, and leave over winter, to germinate the following spring.

Did you know?

The native forests of Scots pine in Scotland are known as the Caledonian Forest. Today, only one per cent of the original forest survives in isolated locations, including Abernethy Forest and Glen Affric.

And in a similar vein...

There are several other pines for you to try

Dwarf mountain pine

'Contorted' Weymouth pine

(R) Montezuma pine

Light green, short, prickly needles. The long cigar-shaped cones contain the smaller seeds

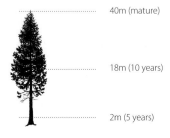

40m (mature)

18m (10 years)

2m (5 years)

Norway Spruce

Picea abies

Norway spruce is a native of Europe, from the mountains of central Europe, to Norway and Greece. Introduced into Britain in 1500, it is mentioned by William Turner in his *Names of Herbes* in 1548. Before the last Ice Age, Norway spruce would probably have grown in Britain, but it never recolonised naturally after the ice retreated.

The species was originally planted for its ornamental value, but 19th-century writers realised the tree had commercial uses, recommending it for spars and masts for ships, scaffolding poles and ladders. As a result the tree began to be planted widely, eg Kielder Forest, in Northumberland. The idea of the Norway spruce as a Christmas tree came to Britain with the Georgian kings in the 17th century, but did not become fashionable until Queen Victoria and Albert were featured in the *Illustrated London News* in 1846.

Widely planted for timber and as an ornamental tree in parks and gardens, Norway spruce likes moist soils and can grow in cold, wet and shallow soils.

Seed guide

Collect the cones from the trees when they have turned from green to brown – usually in October. Keep the cones in a bag or on a dish, at room temperature, to air-dry them. This causes them to open and release their seeds, which should be kept in paper bags until February. Then sow the seeds in pots, covering them with a thin layer of sharp sand, where they should germinate in the spring.

Did you know?

In Europe, spruce fronds were often strewn about the floors of houses (sometimes with juniper), as when crushed underfoot they gave off a refreshing aroma.

And in a similar vein...

There are several other spruces for you to try

Siberian spruce

'Viminalis' Norway spruce

(R) Black spruce

Leaves are broad with almost straight bases. The undersides have white or buff hairs at the vein junctions. The rounded fruit is hairy and faintly ribbed

40m (mature)

20m (10 years)

3m (5 years)

European Lime

Tilia x *europaea*

The origins of this tree are uncertain and it is thought that it may be a hybrid between the small- and large-leaved limes. It may have first been planted in the early 17th century, probably from European stock, and is now widely planted in streets, parks and gardens on a wide range of soils, although it prefers soil that contains lime. However, it is not always the most suitable street tree, as it produces large quantities of basal shoots, which may need annual maintenance.

Like the other two species of lime, the wood was used for carving and clogs, while the under or inner bark (bast) was turned into rope.

Also like the other limes, this tree is excellent for wildlife – hosting 31 insect species – and supports mistletoe. Unlike the other limes, the seed of this species is rarely fertile.

The species prefers a moist loamy alkaline to neutral soil, but will grow on slightly acid soils. It grows poorly on any very dry or very wet soil. European lime tolerates considerable exposure and succeeds in sun or semi-shade.

Seed guide

Lime fruits are a very unusual shape. The clusters of round fruits are attached via stalks to a single, leaf-like bract, which assists wind dispersal. Collect the fruits by hand from the tree after the bracts have turned brown, usually following a frost. Stratify the seeds for one or two winters. Select and sow germinating seeds in spring.

Did you know?

The substance that drips like fine rain in summer from smooth-leaved lime species is honeydew. It is excreted by sap-sucking insects, such as aphids and scale insects. Ants 'farm' the aphids to supplement their diet by collecting the honeydew from them like milk from a cow.

The times they are a-changing

The arboreal landscape we have today has evolved greatly over the centuries. Here's an outline of which trees came to Britain when, and how they've been used.

Pre-Roman era

The relationship between trees and ancient Britons can be deduced from archaeological evidence, mostly unearthed in Mesolithic and Neolithic sites. The evidence shows that timber was used to build dwellings, fashion weapons and tools, and construct stockades or hedges, as well as a source of fuel. Evidence from waste tips reveals that the fruits of wild trees were regularly eaten.

Roman era

The Romans built fine villas and used box to augment their formal gardens. They introduced orchard culture to these shores, planting groves of apples, pears and plums. Romans arriving in Britain brought some of their most useful trees and other plants to support their existence, including sweet chestnut and walnut, and they also introduced stone pine.

Anglo-Saxon era

In Anglo-Saxon charters of the 10th century there are many trees featured, most especially in the hedgerows. Thorn (hawthorn) was most frequently mentioned, while oak features prominently, and also crab apple, willow, elder and alder. Lime, birch and beech, predominantly woodland species, feature much less.

The 16th and 17th centuries

Prior to 1500 there is little information about tree planting or selection of species, but after the Roman withdrawal very few new trees arrived in Britain. It is thought that the sycamore, an inveterate coloniser, arrived from northern Europe some time after the late 13th century, although no date can be specified. Equally, the arrival of the horse chestnut from Turkey around 1600 was the beginning of an entertaining relationship with a characterful tree.

Meanwhile the plant hunters had begun to travel to distant shores. In the mid-16th century the Oriental plane arrived from the Caucasus, and was destined to find fame as the perfect mate for the western plane, one of the earliest arrivals from the Americas in the 1620s. The result – the ubiquitous London plane (above right).

The first hybrid is generally thought to date from 1663 in Britain, and it is highly likely that the cross occurred in the Lambeth garden of the famous 17th-century gardener and plant hunter John Tradescant, as it is known that both species were growing there.

In 1638 the first cedar of Lebanon seed was brought to Britain from Syria by Dr Edward Pococke, and tradition has it that he planted one in his rectory garden at Childrey in Oxfordshire in 1646. The magnificent original tree still thrives.

Throughout the 17th century new trees for Britain continued to cross the Atlantic from eastern and central North America. Arguably, one of the most handsome was the tulip tree, which was admirably suited to the British climate.

The 18th and 19th centuries

The early years of the 19th century saw great collaborations among plant hunters, botanists, nurseries and private collectors. The glorious treasure chest of trees on the west coast of North America still lay untapped, until David Douglas introduced two of Britain's prime timber trees – the

Douglas fir and the Sitka spruce – as well as several other maples, firs and pines.

Archibald Menzies had brought the first monkey puzzles from Chile in 1795, but it was William Lobb who, in 1841, reintroduced the tree and Veitch Nurseries of Exeter popularised it. The monkey puzzle, the cedar and the giant redwood (introduced by Lobb in 1853) became three of the most sought-after specimen trees for impressive centrepieces in many formal gardens.

In the midst of all these exotic importations, the great landscapers, such as Capability Brown, were busily

transforming parks and gardens into vast rolling landscapes, employing man-made 'natural' hills and vales, meandering rivers and tastefully distributed spreading specimen trees or picturesque clumps.

The suburban gardener

With such a vast array of trees now available, it soon became evident that a reliable source of information for planters was required. Landscape gardener John Claudius Loudon was the man to fill this niche. His *Arboretum et Fruticetum Britannicum* of 1838 was a superb reference work for botanists and gardeners alike. Loudon went out of his way to champion the widespread planting of all the new and varied species from around the world.

By the end of the 18th century, churchyards in urban areas could not accommodate the numbers of dead from the increased urban population. Parliament therefore authorised new commercial cemeteries. The first was established in Liverpool in 1825. Loudon promoted the idea that these new cemeteries could become botanical gardens for the education of all classes of society. At Abney Park (1840), the trees and shrubs were labelled and it was considered to be the most comprehensive arboretum in London.

The 20th century to today

The Victorians made important moves in towns and cities to provide green spaces in rapidly expanding conurbations. Public parks were planted and streets were lined with trees. Unfortunately, by the second half of the 19th century, the effects of air pollution were beginning to have an increasingly deleterious effect on the new tree planting.

Reacting to the effects of increasing urbanisation, Ebenezer Howard formulated the concept of the Garden City in 1902. Howard's idea was to integrate the built and natural environments more closely. The first new town, Letchworth (1904), was inspired by this concept and was planned around the preservation of existing woods, trees and hedges, along with extensive tree planting. Initially, an attempt was made to plant a distinctive species for each new road. For example, almond and red horse chestnut were planted for different streets. The town square was planted with hornbeam (above), deodar cedar, common beech, Lombardy poplar and Cornish elm.

Garden Cities and new towns

As the concept of the Garden City gradually evolved, new styles of planting emerged in the suburbs, such as planting grass verges with small trees. This was possible because a number of smaller varieties had become available, including Japanese cherries and purple plums. Government housing design manuals of the inter-war period (eg the 'Tudor Walters Report' of 1919), suggested that trees should be placed 'in positions suitable to the size of their ultimate growth'.

The authors were concerned to avoid the constant need for pruning of forest-sized trees planted in confined spaces. However, to have created the space necessary for such large trees would have meant reducing house densities to lower levels than were recommended at the time. The smaller cherry trees thus provided the planners with a species which seemed to suit the new requirements of these towns and were widely used.

The 1980s and 1990s saw a number of developments which have focused attention on the numerous benefits which trees provide in towns. The development of new towns has provided the opportunity to design and plan large areas of tree planting within the urban fabric, to the extent that Milton Keynes and Telford have called themselves 'Forest Towns'.

Green lungs of the city

The existence of large tracts of derelict land in declining industrial areas has provided the opportunity for large-scale planting projects in cities such as Birmingham, Belfast, St Helens and Edinburgh. Associated with this trend has been the growth in interest in the concept of urban forestry, which regards all the trees in an urban area as comprising a 'forest' and manages them for the many benefits they can give, from visual amenity to timber.

In rural Britain tree planting had long been part of the country calendar. Hedge trees were planted or encouraged in order to provide timber, fuel wood, protection and shade. Orchard culture was brisk, with a good demand for fruit, cider and perry manufacture, and even the need for vegetable dyes, provided by fruits such as the damson.

However, after the war there was a progressive move towards intensive agriculture, which saw field systems drastically enlarged at the expense of many hedges and their large trees. Orchards began to be less profitable and government subsidies meant the land could be used for better returns. The demise of traditional orchards continues to this day.

Elsewhere matters seem a lot brighter. The work of many Tree Council members and others has engendered an ever-increasing interest and understanding of trees and their care. The boundless energy and enthusiasm of The Tree Council's volunteer Tree Wardens has also increased tree awareness and a sense of custodianship and pride of trees in local communities across Britain.

When did they get here?

A quick guide to the arrival in Britain of common tree species.

The term 'native tree' is given to species that colonised the British Isles naturally after the last Ice Age (around 10,000 years ago) and before these islands were cut off from the rest of Europe by the rising sea levels.

The 33 species in the list opposite are usually quoted as native trees.

Curiously, however, usually omitted from this list are Plymouth pear and wild pear, which would bring the total to 35. Then there are 16 other species of rare and endemic (found only in the UK) whitebeams, which are seldom counted but which would take the total to 51.

The true service tree – which is probably a native based on an isolated colony found growing on the cliffs of South Wales – would make 52.

In addition, there are the willows – which most people regard as shrubs but for the purposes of this book are trees – which would take the total to 66. Other plants which are usually thought of as shrubs, but which we again call trees for the purpose of this book, would take the total to 76.

Finally, there are a few trees and shrubs whose origins are confused, such as barberry, English elm, sycamore and white elm.

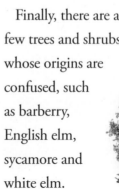

Native trees

Alder, ash, aspen, bay willow, beech, bird cherry, black poplar, box, common oak, crab apple, crack willow, downy birch, field maple, goat willow, hawthorn, hazel, holly, hornbeam, juniper, large-leaved lime, Midland hawthorn, rowan, Scots pine, sessile oak, silver birch, small-leaved lime, strawberry tree, whitebeam, white willow, wild cherry, wild service tree, wych elm and yew.

Rare and endemic whitebeams

Sorbus anglica, Sorbus arranensis, Sorbus bristoliensis, Sorbus devoniensis, Sorbus eminens, Sorbus hibernica, Sorbus lancastriensis, Sorbus leptophylla, Sorbus leyana, Sorbus minima, Sorbus porrigentiformis, Sorbus pseudofennica, Sorbus rupicola, Sorbus subcuneata, Sorbus vexans and *Sorbus wilmottiana*.

Willows

Almond willow, common sallow, creeping willow, dark-leaved willow, downy willow, dwarf willow, eared willow, mountain willow, net-leaved willow, osier, purple willow, tea-leaved willow, whortle-leaved willow and woolly willow.

Shrubs

Alder buckthorn, blackthorn, dogwood, dwarf birch, elder, guelder rose, purging buckthorn, sea buckthorn, spindle and wayfaring tree.

Introductions

Roman introductions 1st to 4th century AD

Stone pine, sweet chestnut, walnut, and possibly English elm, medlar, mulberry and fig (evidence of the last three has been found in a few Roman sites, but whether they were planting the trees or eating imported fruit is uncertain).

There is a large historical gap until written evidence begins. Then:

16th century or earlier

Sycamore, black and white mulberry, holm oak, Oriental plane, white cedar, tamarisk, Judas tree and laburnum.

17th century

Norway spruce, European larch, tulip tree, false acacia, horse chestnut (1616), Norway maple (1638), swamp cypress (c1640), cedar of Lebanon (1646), red maple (1656) and London plane (1663).

18th century

Copper beech, Indian bean tree (1726), weeping willow (1730), turkey oak (1735), tree of heaven (1751), ginkgo (1754), Corsican pine (1758), zelkova (1760), golden rain tree (1763), rhododendron (ponticum) (1763), cricket bat willow (1780), Irish yew (c1780) and monkey puzzle (1795).

19th century

Douglas fir (1827), deodar cedar (1830), noble fir (1830), grand fir (1830), Sitka spruce (1831), Monterey pine (1831), coast redwood (1843), giant redwood (1853), katsura tree (1864) and Leyland cypress (natural hybrid found in Welshpool in 1888).

20th century

Dawn redwood (1941) and various eucalyptus.

21st century

Wollemi pine (2004).

So, you'd like to become a Tree Warden?

If you're enjoying growing trees from seed, then why not take the next step. Become a Tree Warden and champion your local trees.

If you've been reading the Tree Wardens' tales in the pages of this book, you'll know that the role has something for everyone. Whatever your experience, your interests and the amount of time you can spare, you too can become one of the many enthusiasts around the country that help to make such a difference to the nation's trees.

Got any questions? The following page should help.

So what exactly is The Tree Council's Tree Warden Scheme all about?

In a nutshell, it's a national initiative that enables people to play an active role in conserving and enhancing their local trees and woods. The Tree Council founded the scheme in 1990 and currently coordinates it with the support of National Grid and the government department Communities and Local Government.

What do Tree Wardens do?

Tree Wardens are volunteers, appointed by parish councils or other community organisations, who gather information about their local trees, get involved in local tree matters and carry out practical projects to do with trees and woods.

Are there many Tree Wardens out there?

There are now over 8,000 Tree Wardens in 140 networks across the country. Not only does joining the scheme give you the chance to do something for your local trees, it also puts you in touch with like-minded people in your area. Many lifetime friendships are made through involvement with the Tree Warden Scheme.

OK, I'm hooked. How can I come on board?

New Tree Wardens are always welcome and the first step for anyone interested in volunteering is to find out if there is a local network and then to contact the coordinator.

The Tree Warden Scheme networks in England, Wales, Scotland and the Channel Islands are listed at www.treecouncil.org.uk, with details of local contacts.

Anyone thinking of starting a new local Tree Warden network – urban or rural – should contact The Tree Council for advice and support.

Read all about it

If your appetite's whetted for more natural history, then don't disappoint it. There's plenty here to read and inspire you to even greater heights.

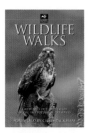

Wildlife Walks

A unique walking guide to over 500 of the most beautiful nature reserves in the UK, complete with contact details, maps and wildlife guides. Published in association with The Wildlife Trusts.
£14.99 Think Books (www.think-books.com)

Birds in Your Garden

Expert advice on attracting birds into your garden, illustrated with gorgeous photography, and full of great ideas. Published in association with The Wildlife Trusts.
£12.99 Think Books (www.think-books.com)

Wildlife Gardening for Everyone

A compendium of answers to over 200 need-to-know questions about cultivating wildlife in your garden. With expert advice from professional RHS gardeners and Wildlife Trust naturalists.
£12.99 Think Books (www.think-books.com)

Wildlife Britain

The essential full-colour guide to discovering and enjoying over 1,000 of the best wildlife sites in the UK. Includes specialist commentary from organisations such as Natural England, RSPB, Wildfowl & Wetlands Trust and The Wildlife Trusts.
£12.99 Think Books (www.think-books.com)

Going, Going, Gone?

One hundred animals and plants that are specifically identified by the conservation organisations of the world as most under threat, and what needs to be done in order to save them.
£9.99 Think Books (www.think-books.com)

Carbon Jargon

A handy little book that addresses the key myths and criticisms of carbon-related environmental issues in a simple Q and A format.
£4.99 Think Books (www.think-books.com)

The Heritage Trees of Britain & Northern Ireland

Combining striking full-colour photography with a range of archival sources, Jon Stokes and Donald Rodger bring to life for a new generation the rich history surrounding these living treasures.

£16.99 The Tree Council (www.treecouncil.org.uk)

The Hedge Tree Handbook

Part of the Hedge Tree Campaign, a national initiative by The Tree Council in partnership with National Grid. It aims to protect hedge trees and nurture new ones to ensure there is no net loss of hedge trees in the UK.

£6.99 The Tree Council (www.treecouncil.org.uk)

Trees in Your Ground

Aims to help everyone to value the trees growing in their neighbourhoods, plant more trees in their gardens and to work with others to get more trees planted at work, school, along streets, in neighbouring gardens and in public or private parks.

£7.99 The Tree Council (www.treecouncil.org.uk)

Why are Leaves Green?

A colourful guide to everything you ever wanted to know about trees. Answers to many frequently asked questions about trees, such as: When should I prune my trees? Which is the world's oldest tree? Does ivy kill trees?

£9.99 The Tree Council (www.treecouncil.org.uk)

Heritage Trees of Scotland

Packed with the most stunning photographs, this book features 134 trees from all over Scotland and highlights the country's most special trees. Produced in conjunction with the Forestry Commission Scotland.

£19.99 The Tree Council (www.treecouncil.org.uk)

Grower's notes

Jays and squirrels are notorious for burying their acorns and other booty, then forgetting where they left them. Don't be like the squirrels: use these pages to record where and when you planted your seeds, and to monitor their progress.

Grower's notes

Grower's notes

Grower's notes

Grower's notes

Grower's notes